Transgressors

Transgressors

Toward a Feminist Biblical Theology

Claudia Janssen, Ute Ochtendung, and Beate Wehn,
editors

Translated by Linda M. Maloney

A Michael Glazier Book

THE LITURGICAL PRESS
Collegeville, Minnesota

www.litpress.org

A Michael Glazier Book published by The Liturgical Press.

Cover design by Ann Blattner. Illustration: PhotoDisc.

Originally published as *GrenzgängerInnen: unterwegs zu einer anderen biblischen Theologie: ein feministisch-theologisches Lesebuch* © 1999 Matthias-Grünewald Verlag, Mainz.

1   2   3   4   5   6   7   8   9

Library of Congress Cataloging-in-Publication Data

GrenzgängerInnen. English.
    Transgressors : toward a feminist biblical theology / Claudia Janssen, Ute Ochtendung, and Beate Wehn, editors ; translated by Linda M. Maloney.
       p. cm.
    Festschrift for Luise Schottroff.
    "A Michael Glazier book."
    Includes bibliographical references and index.
    ISBN 0-8146-5094-5 (alk. paper)
      1. Bible—Feminist criticism. 2. Feminist theology. I. Janssen, Claudia. II. Ochtendung, Ute. III. Wehn, Beate. IV. Schottroff, Luise. V. Title.

BS521.4 .G7413 2002
230'.082—dc21

2001050266

For Luise Schottroff
on her sixty-fifth birthday

Transgressing Women
Luise and the Others

you went ahead of us
crossing borders
—that they were closed was something we first learned
from you, a sense gained in painful glimpses
you showed us:
the longing for elbow room beyond the borders
and Lydia's impatience
these brought into being lands past and yet to come
in which there is little of milk and honey flowing
and we are not promised myriad descendants
but lands
in which before us women and men
have believed and thought with all their senses
and shared the bread of days past
rather than let it turn to stone, stamped and measured
and declared their own possession
to be greedily hoarded

you planted your seed in yet harder ground
than we till today
your work and hope
the voices of countless women
our curiosity
and the unfolding power that dwells within it
these you brought to bloom
through all the times of drought
and later to bitter and delicious fruit
that renews itself
today and tomorrow
in wondrous ways

when we set out
you did not tell us
which roads led to the goal
but you gave us suspicion as our compass and
longing for fullness of life as our horizon
and food for the journey
so again and again we found others at our side
and we told each other
about Hannah and Mary, the woman baking bread,
and Ruth
whom you, already before us, had awakened to new life

the courage of these our predecessors
and the fact that you did not give up
in spite of the stones in your path
make it possible for us to continue on

what we shall be
has not yet appeared
but we would not be it at all without you
teachers of God
transgressor women
taboo breakers
and healers
not without those who come after us
and not without God
who makes us ready to break forth.

Christiane Rösener

Contents

Foreword   xiii

Christiane Rösener
"Your People Shall Be My People, and Your God My God."
The Shared Life of Ruth and Naomi as a
Model for Women Transgressing Intercultural Boundaries   1

Stefanie Müller
Living with the Torah. A Conversation with Rabbi Beruriah   9

Beate Wehn
"I Am a Handmaid of the Living God!"
The Apostle Thecla and the Consequences of Transgression   19

Claudia Janssen
Paul: Walking the Line Between Traditions and Ages   31

Marlene Crüsemann
Living Water:
Elements of a Feminist Proclamation According to John 4   39

Dagmar Henze
Peter: A Transgressor in His Own Time   47

Irene Dannemann
The Slave Woman's Challenge to Peter   53

Sigrid Lampe-Densky
Domitia, Marcia, and the Nameless Smuggler:
Pearl Dealers in the Roman Empire   59

Luzia Sutter Rehmann
The *Agunah,* the Bound Wife:
A Transgressive Woman in Jewish Law and
Her Significance for Early Christian Communities   67

Sigrun Wetzlaugk
"Do Justice for Me!"   77

Ivoni Richter Reimer
Life Calls for Triumph and Celebration   87

Choon-Ho You-Martin
"Women's Movements" and "Women's Theology."
Social Change in South Korea between
Tradition and Postmodernity   97

Eske Wollrad
On Getting Out of One's Skin:
Depictions of White Femininity in Film   111

Ulrike Metternich
"*Dynamis* and Womanpower."
An Investigation of the Concept of *dynamis* in the
Gospels and Paul   121

Martina S. Gnadt
"What we will be has not yet been revealed."
An Archaeology of Seeing in John 9   127

Hanna Kreisel-Liebermann
Protecting and Holding:
Pastoral Companionship for
Cancer Patients in a Multidisciplinary Team   137

Andrea Bieler
Written in Their Bodies:
On the Significance of Rituals in Caring for AIDS Patients   145

Wilhelm Schwendemann
God's Answer to Job   155

Bettina Eltrop
Problem Girls:
A Transgressive Reading of the
Parable of the Ten Virgins (Matthew 25:1-13)   163

Author Biographies   173

Index of Subjects   179

Foreword

Transgressor: the word applies to women and men who live and act across the grain of traditional religious and social currents of their own time. These are people who go their own way, questioning the status quo and thus challenging traditions and trusted patterns of thinking.

In this book we have gone in search of them, becoming acquainted with unknown women and men of biblical times and looking from a different angle at those already known. People who transgress boundaries and encourage others to do the same can be found today also, in our churches and universities, in all the corners of our lives. We aim to sketch the traditions of resistant, inconvenient, courageous women and men from ancient times to today. Of course these sketches will only be brief and by way of examples, because their history is complex and resists any kind of reduction to a single pattern. Each of the persons depicted here stands only for herself or himself, and yet is also within the continuity of biblical tradition, which for them was a source of strength and an impetus to be different.

The book is also a gift of thanks to a transgressive woman of our own time, on her birthday: on April 11, 1999 our teacher, colleague, and friend Luise Schottroff turned 65. We, the women and men of her doctoral seminar, want in this way to thank her for years of critical support, scholarly companionship, and solidarity.

In her writing Luise Schottroff has repeatedly shown how productive and enjoyable it can be to set out in new directions and thereby to transgress boundaries: between antiquity and the present, between scholarship and pastoral practice, between Jewish and Christian traditions, between different countries and cultures, and not least between women and men. She knows how to infect others with her enthusiasm for biblical texts, and how to convey the immediacy of these traditions. The variety of resistant thought and social praxis expressed in the people described in this book also reflects the openness and joy in discovery that mark the context within which Luise Schottroff works.

The apostle Thecla, the rabbi Beruriah, Ruth and Naomi, Peter, Paul, Job, the Samaritan woman at the well, a nameless slave woman, unbending widows and wise virgins, merchant women—Jewish and early Christian transgressors—stand in continuity with women and men in various contexts in our contemporary world: in Germany, Brazil, and South Korea. It is evident that in comparison to biblical times the concrete circumstances of life have changed, but not the fundamental confrontation with the meaning of justice and human dignity in each of these life-contexts: Jesus' encounter with the Samaritan at the well requires us to reflect anew on our understanding of liberating proclamation; biblical stories of healing can inspire reflection on how we deal with illness, and how we encounter people who suffer from AIDS or cancer; economic injustice, racism, and anti-Judaism are challenges to us, evoking prophetic critique, stubborn resistance, and courageous action.

The transgressive people depicted here invite us to join company with them, and so to discover anew the immediacy of biblical traditions in our own time.

Claudia Janssen
Ute Ochtendung
Beate Wehn

Kassel, Germany
January 1999

Christiane Rösener

"Your People Shall Be My People, and Your God My God." The Shared Life of Ruth and Naomi as a Model for Women Transgressing Intercultural Boundaries

Feminist theology rediscovered history long ago. The novella about Ruth and her mother-in-law, Naomi, is one of the first stories of women to be retrieved from oblivion by other women since the 1970s. It is familiar to a great many women: because of a famine in Bethlehem, Elimelech and his wife Naomi flee to Moab. Soon afterward, Elimelech dies. Naomi remains there alone with her two sons. The sons grow up and marry two Moabite women, Orpah and Ruth. After ten years the sons also die. After that, Naomi sets out to return to Judah, where the famine has ceased. She advises her two daughters-in-law to return to their mothers and remarry, but neither of the two wants to separate from Naomi. At length Orpah agrees to return, but Ruth remains with her mother-in-law. The two travel together to Bethlehem, where they live by gleaning in the fields of the wealthy. But then they succeed in bringing a close relative of Elimelech, a landowner named Boaz, to accept responsibility and marry Ruth. This ensures that Naomi will also be cared for. Ruth becomes pregnant and bears a son for Naomi to raise.

It is obvious why this story has become a favorite of feminist theology: it is one of the few biblical stories in which women's friendship is central. Here the fidelity of a young woman to an older woman becomes a model of faith. In a church and a theology in which women are still shoved to the margins and in which marriage is still exalted as the most important form of relationship this woman-centered story can reinforce our faith and our relationships with other women.

But how close could the two women really have been? Were not the cultures from which they came too different? Did they not believe in different gods before Ruth accepted Naomi's God? Did the one not

1

remain always a stranger in the other's country? And was Ruth not required to completely renounce her own culture in order to follow Naomi?

These questions, which consider the narrative from the standpoint of the encounter of two women of different cultures, have only recently surfaced in feminist interpretation. They are similar to the questions that preoccupy women who are seeking opportunities for dialogue with feminist theologians in other cultural contexts. Linda A. Moody, a white American theologian, has suggested that we take the story of Ruth and Naomi as a guide for (theological) encounters between women in different contexts and cultures (cf. Moody 1996). She sees the shared life of Ruth and Naomi as a biblical model for an intercultural encounter between feminist theologies that is woman-centered and liberating, bodily and relational (cf. Moody 1996, 2). In what follows I would like to pursue her suggestion and its possible implications for a feminist intercultural theology by reading the story of Ruth and Naomi through new eyes.

Coexistence:
A Model for Transgressing Intercultural Boundaries [1]

In rereading the book of Ruth I am guided by a concept that describes a special kind of intercultural encounter: the concept of coexistence. The missiologist and student of comparative religions Theo Sundermeier adopted this concept from the "base communities" in Latin America to describe the common life of people in a community marked above all by three characteristics:

- the members of the community support one another in social hardships, illness, and death;

- they learn with and from one another;

- they celebrate together (cf. Sundermeier 1986b, 66).

Sundermeier applies the concept of coexistence, drawn originally from ecclesiology, to the community of people from different cultures, and especially from North and South. He sees the model of coexistence as an opportune replacement for the still-current model of encounter

---

[1] Translator's note: references to Sundermeier's work consistently translate his word *Konvivenz* with "coexistence." The word has unfortunate Cold War associations in English, but we use it here for the sake of harmony with other works. A neologism like "convivience" might be preferable.

called "pro-existence," the relationship of "being for others," between people of the North and the South. The model of pro-existence builds on the inequality of givers and recipients and does not aim to break down borders (cf. Sundermeier 1986a, 14). In contrast, the concept of coexistence suggests a common life of people from North and South that is conscious of their interdependence.

Sundermeier sees the biblical foundation for God's will to coexistence in both the First and Second Testaments. Thus the Exodus tradition in the First Testament is pointed above all toward the dwelling of God's people in the land of promise, so that they may till it and live together in peace, with God in their midst (cf. Sundermeier 1986b, 67–69). In this way its aim is a life formed by coexistence. In the Second Testament Jesus is sent to dwell, as the Word of God, among human beings. His life with the disciples and his festal meals with the rejected of society are models of coexistence (ibid. 69–71). Ultimately this is continued in the community of Christians in the Acts of the Apostles, where people learned together, used their goods to help one another, and celebrated together in the Lord's Supper the feast of his resurrection (cf. Acts 2:42-47).

A coexistence thus understood implies for the encounter of different cultures that a common daily life in which the stranger-partners get better acquainted with each other is more important than an ecumenical dialogue of selected delegates at a conference. This is because coexistence aims at more than an accidental, brief encounter. Its intention is rather an enduring and spatial union, because only common experience of the whole of life can effect a change of consciousness (cf. Sundermeier 1986b, 51).

Sundermeier's concept of coexistence is persuasive because of its wholistic understanding of ecumenical learning. It makes the limitations of a purely verbal dialogue quite clear. But it also poses the question of feasibility: can there be such a thing? It is, after all, impossible for everyone to leave her or his country and journey to other lands in order to become better acquainted with the strangers there. But before we pursue this question and ask whether coexistence is a feasible model for us, I would first like to trace the coexistence of Ruth and Naomi in order to test whether the concept Sundermeier has introduced can help us to describe their intercultural common life.

The Community of Ruth and Naomi:
A Case of Coexistence

In what follows I will consider the story of Ruth and Naomi under the following aspects of coexistence:

(a) Ruth and Naomi's decision to coexist,

(b) their mutual care and concern,

(c) their learning together, and

(d) the possibility of identity and community.

(a) Ruth and Naomi's Decision to Coexist

Ruth and Naomi decide, on the basis of their mutual affection, to live together; in doing so, they secure their own survival. They reinforce their decision by making a covenant, reflecting the character of the covenant-making God of Israel. As God has promised: "I will be your God and you will be my people," so these two women promise to share one people and one God (cf. Moody 1996, 149). With this covenant they break through the barriers of family and cultural-religious allegiance. Culturally they had never before belonged to one community. On the contrary: they come from two different countries in each of which there were notable prejudices against the other. For example, in Israel Moab was considered hostile, sexually perverse, and unjust (cf. Levine 1992, 80). Their family relationship ended with the death of Ruth's husband, or would have ended, at the latest, when Ruth married again. Nevertheless, the two women decide to stay together. Ruth promises to take Naomi, her people, and her God for her own, and not to allow herself to be parted from Naomi by anything but death. After some hesitation, Naomi accepts Ruth's decision and thus agrees to the covenant. From then on, Ruth the Moabite belongs inseparably to Naomi's family: she lovingly calls her "my daughter" (cf., for example, 1:11; 2:2, 22; 3:1), and she twice describes Boaz as their common relative (2:20; 3:2). At the end of the story the neighbors even say that Ruth is worth more to Naomi than seven sons (4:15). That is the most extreme expression of the breaking down of barriers, and not only because, contrary to the values of the time, a daughter is esteemed more highly than a son. Here the non-physical, foreign daughter is worth more than seven sons, the covenant between two women of different cultures more important than physical motherhood of many sons. Through Ruth's decision to leave her country and her family, but also through Naomi's opening her own family and culture for Ruth, the two women transgress the boundaries of their respective cultures and thus mutually contribute to the fulfillment of their covenant: in this way Naomi's people can become Ruth's people as well.

(b) Mutual Care and Concern

Mutual care in sorrow and material poverty is a sustaining element in Ruth and Naomi's common life. This begins in Moab, where Naomi lives from the love and care of her daughters-in-law (cf. 1:8b). In Bethlehem Ruth, as the younger and stronger of the two, provides at first for their common necessities by gleaning at the harvest. Later Naomi thinks of a plan by which they can obtain secure support: Ruth's marriage to Boaz. They can only carry out this plan together. Naomi's cunning, her knowledge of culture and customs, and her family relationships are as necessary in this case as Ruth's beauty and her ability to attract Boaz. In the end this marriage guarantees a secure future for both of them. Even after the wedding Ruth and Naomi's care for one another continues in their mutual care for Ruth's son Obed, whom Naomi will bring up. The neighbors tell us this when, at the naming festival, they say: "a son has been born to Naomi" (4:17).

(c) Learning Together

In the course of the story Ruth and Naomi have to learn a great deal. Both of them have to come to terms with their suffering and the difficulties of living in a strange place. In this they are able to learn together and from each other. We can only guess how this learning process looked: Did Naomi tell Ruth about her people's experience on their way to the Promised Land? Did they show each other how to prepare simple dishes from the wild herbs and grains that grew in their respective countries? The development of the women in the course of the narrative, as both take a more and more active role in shaping their lives, shows us at any rate *that* Ruth and Naomi learned together: despite death and bitterness they are able to continue living in community. For Ruth there is still another kind of learning, that is, acquiring a strange cultural language. With her covenant she commits herself to a lifetime of learning a strange culture that will never be as familiar to her as her own, a culture in which she will always remain "the Moabite." In her learning process she depends on Naomi's help and explanations. But in Moab she, in turn, must have helped Naomi to learn the culture of her native land; thus at different points in their common life each of the women was either a teacher or a learner.

(d) The Possibility of Identity and Community

Naomi and Ruth enter into community with people of a foreign culture. Both leave their native country. Naomi remains almost ten years in Moab, while Ruth, according to the story, presumably lives in Bethlehem until her death. In this way each woman becomes familiar with a different culture and different religious traditions. Both form close relationships with the people of their second "homeland," but they also experience strangeness and alienation in the unfamiliar culture. In this way they learn that it is possible to retain a bit of homeland even among strangers. The foreign place will never be fully home to them: after the death of her family, Naomi leaves Moab. Ruth, too, remains a stranger in Judah, although through her mother-in-law and her marriage to Boaz she is increasingly integrated: throughout the text she is described as "the Moabite." The fact that both women remain foreigners means, on the one hand, that they have to learn to live with the painful sense of being different and separated from their own roots. But it also means that they preserve their own identity in the encounter with the other culture, and are not melted into it.

Despite the ways in which their experiences are comparable, Ruth's definitive departure from her homeland represents a clearer break with her cultural and religious home than does Naomi's. She takes a radical step out of her own culture, as no one else in Israel's history since Abraham had done. But Abraham was called by God to do so, and a land and progeny were promised to him (cf. Trible 1993, 193). Ruth only followed Naomi and the strength of their mutual covenant. Anyone who has lived for a long period of time in a strange land knows how much courage such a step requires, but also how much loneliness is involved. Does she entirely abandon her own culture and her own gods? We do not know. Perhaps her life in the foreign land gave her a keener sense of her own roots. Perhaps she suffered from the separation from her culture and from her limited communication with people in the new country. Did she find that her community of life with Naomi offered sufficient compensation? Perhaps she also found opportunities to remain faithful to her own culture and religious origins, for while the text speaks of Ruth's confession of YHWH it does not say explicitly that she turned away from her own gods. Perhaps her covenantal promise is primarily an expression of deep respect for Naomi's culture and religion, and is not the same thing as a conversion. It may be that in Ruth's thinking God had many names and was not restricted to a single culture. We cannot give a clear answer to these questions, but we can come somewhat closer to an answer in our own experiences of coexistence.

From the perspective of coexistence it is clear that the book of Ruth describes a community of life between two women from different cultures who unite their lives, their learning, and their suffering, their joy and their God, despite and in the face of all differences. The two women do this in the awareness that they must rely on one another, but also out of a deep love for each other. This love between Ruth and Naomi, which motivates them to form their covenant, is an important aspect of their coexistence. I would thus add personal union between individuals to the elements of coexistence suggested by Sundermeier. The possibilities and the limitations of coexistence can only be experienced through personal connections, and only in this way can it change individuals.

The difficulties that stand in the way of coexistence between people of different cultures are also difficult to grasp in terms of Sundermeier's concept—for example, power differentials, misunderstandings, loneliness. For Ruth and Naomi we can only suspect these, for the idyl of the narrative reveals little of such things. In light of our present-day experiences of transgressing intercultural boundaries, we need to examine these difficulties a little more closely.

Ruth and Naomi's Covenant as a Challenge to Intercultural Encounters between Women

It would be a violation of the literary character of the book of Ruth to try to derive a directly transferable model for a present-day coexistence of women from the common life of Ruth and Naomi. Nevertheless, the narrative can, at several points, challenge us to such coexistence. I find Ruth and Naomi's covenant, the mutual promise of coexistence with which they begin their common life, an especially fruitful point of reference.

According to Linda A. Moody such a covenant could be the basis for a contemporary theological dialogue between women in different contexts: "If women from differing cultural contexts accept the notion that God is a covenanting God who can bring together women from very different cultural backgrounds, such as Ruth and Naomi, we have a possible basis for mutual, shared theological reflection across the boundaries of difference" (Moody 1996, 4). One motivation for us in making such a covenant can be the knowledge that our survival on this earth is only possible together; another is the desire for mutual learning from our different theologies, as well as trust in the expansiveness of a common God who liberates all of us. Our goal is not to veil the differences between women and to declare prematurely that there is sisterhood between women all over the world. We come from different cultures and contexts, and it is very important to make those differences visible. Ruth and Naomi's covenant did not reduce their cultural differences to the same level. Ruth's promise: "Your people shall be my people, and your God my God" did not anticipate a situation that denied her origins, but obligated her to ongoing learning from the other, and thus to a deep respect for her culture and religion. We, too, with such a covenant may underscore our desire for a relationship that rests on mutuality and justice, and give expression to our will to fill that covenant with life through friendship and hard work (cf. Moody 1996, 4).

Hard work will not be lacking, for despite our longing for mutuality there are many obstacles to a (theological) dialogue across the boundaries of cultures. We come from countries that hold different positions in the economic power relationships of this world order. We are blind to our own complicity in the oppression of other women. We often find it difficult to break through our own worldviews. We are in danger of subsuming others when we write their slogans on our own banners. In light of all these difficulties it often seems easier to keep silent than to seek dialogue. At this very point it can be useful to seek points of opening for a coexistence with other women that goes beyond mere dialogue: We can seek contact with women of different cultures and different faiths in our own country. In the framework of community partnerships we can covenant with women of other countries, or work together on concrete points at which our lives, so apparently distant, in fact touch one another: for example, trade in products that are produced in one country and sold in another. We can read feminist theologies written in other cultural contexts and try to connect them with our own lives. Some individuals can seize the opportunity to live with women in another country for an extended period of time and to learn with them.

There are many opportunities for taking our longing for one another and our knowledge that women here and there belong together so seriously that, like Ruth and Naomi, we arrange all our affairs accordingly. They are waiting for us to discover them. Only in that way can we, trusting in the covenanting God, become people who transgress the line between cultures.

Bibliography

Levine, Amy-Jill. "Ruth," in Carol Newsom and Sharon H. Ringe, eds., *The Women's Bible Commentary*. Louisville: Westminster/John Knox, 1992, 78–84.

Moody, Linda A. *Women Encounter God. Theology Across the Boundaries of Difference*. Maryknoll, N.Y.: Orbis, 1996.

Sundermeier, Theo. "Sich verändern durch Zusammenleben. Konvivenz zwischen Nord und Süd," *Evangelische Kommentare* 19 (1986) 14–16 (= 1986a).

_____. "Konvivenz als Grundstruktur ökumenischer Existenz heute," in Wolfgang Huber, Dietrich Ritschl, and Theo Sundermeier, *Ökumenische Existenz heute*. Munich, 1986, 49–100 (= 1986b).

Trible, Phyllis. *God and the Rhetoric of Sexuality*. Philadelphia: Fortress, 1978.

Stefanie Müller

Living with the Torah.
A Conversation with Rabbi Beruriah

We are in Palestine, in the second century of the Common Era. I am en route to Tiberias to visit a woman who has become rather controversial in Jewish tradition. Around the next curve we ought to be able to see the city. Yes, there it is: Tiberias, a handsome city, beautifully situated on the Sea of Gennesareth. The morning mist is gently rising into the upper air. Even from this distance I can see the palace, the temple, and the stadium. Herod Antipas built them all at the beginning of the first century: a Hellenistic *polis* in honor of the emperor Tiberius. Since the city was built over gravesites and Jewish people, as a result, did not want to live there, they were moved here by force. Hence the larger part of the population is of Jewish origin, in sharp contrast to other Greek metropolises. After the Bar Kochba revolt Tiberias became one of the more important cities, because Galilee suffered less damage in the war than Judea. Tiberias also became one of the most important focuses of Jewish scholarship and learning, and not only because the Sanhedrin and the Patriarchate settled there in the third century. Here most of the work was done on the collection and completion of the Tannaitic and Amoraitic writings, including the Mishnah and the Jerusalem Talmud as a whole.

But now back to the scene of our story. During this short excursus about Tiberias I have reached the city wall and entered through its gate. Although it is still early morning there are already a good many people about. That is not surprising because, for one thing, people here have to make good use of the morning hours since in the course of the day it gets very hot here on the Sea of Gennesareth; moreover, there is a lot of work for people to do if they are to make a living. Most of the people are agricultural workers, growers of grain, wine grapes, olives, and sometimes fruit and vegetables. Others are shepherds, and here on the lake there are a lot of fisherfolk. As I pass through the city I encounter the greatest possible variety of artisans' shops: here a blacksmith, there a pottery, and so on. What the people produce is just barely enough to support their daily existence. Consequently it is a matter of course, and absolutely necessary, that women also work outside their homes.

Ah, that building on the next corner must be the house of study, the *Bet ha Midrash,* founded by Rabbi Meir, a student of Rabbi Akiba, one of the greatest halakhic authorities of his time and the husband of the woman I want to visit. The house of study is a simple, square, flat-roofed building with very few windows. This is where the famous sages, learned in the Torah, meet. I am already excited. I knock on the door—no one answers, so I enter uninvited. It is dark; I can see only a single candle in the corner. As my eyes become accustomed to the dim light I make out a person standing at a lectern, murmuring. Perhaps I am in the wrong place, after all, for I would expect to find here a group of scholars holding discussions with their students. I approach cautiously. The dimly-perceived person is wearing a broad robe and a white scarf. When I am a few feet away I clear my throat and ask: "Excuse me; where can I find Rabbi Beruriah?" The figure turns swiftly around, checks me from top to toe, and says: "The one you seek stands before you. Shalom! You are welcome in our house of study."

I can scarcely believe it, but there she really is, before me: Beruriah, the only woman cited in rabbinic literature as a teacher of the Law. I bow before her and clear my throat again. "Shalom, Rabbi Beruriah. How is it that I find you here alone in the house of study?"

"How do you imagine that the scholars and their families live? It is true that the Torah and the scrolls of the Scriptures are the center of our lives, but we can't eat them. Most of us pursue normal activities, just like non-scholars. I myself would be in the fields, too, but I was expecting to meet you."

"That is truly kind of you. I just wanted to ask, though: In the period of the Second Temple it was a different matter, was it not?—I mean as far as scholars doing manual labor is concerned."

"Oh, well, when our predecessors could still work as scribes in the Temple and were responsible for the writing and interpretation of the Torah they received financial support. But that was a long time ago. From about the third century before your reckoning onward the scholars separated from the Temple and founded their own houses of study, which were also open to other groups. In that way all could interpret the Torah as long as they had the necessary intellectual and moral qualifications."

"Excuse me for interrupting, but when you say 'all,' no doubt you mean 'all men,' and only those who had enough money to afford the luxury of studying Torah?"

"That is not quite true. As I was just trying to explain, even scholars had to pursue normal activity. Only a few were able to live from their work as scribes. And as far as women are concerned, which it seems is at the heart of your question—take a look at me, am I not a woman?"

"Of course, of course, only I thought . . . ." Her directness reduced me to confusion.

"You are not entirely wrong. It is not easy for a woman to gain entry into these sacred halls. Like the people around us, we live in a patriarchal society with its own laws and structures, one that shows women and men what their place is. But for the most part reality is different from what, for example, the rabbis later wrote in the Talmud, which you probably have read. As far as my own situation is concerned, I can say that generations came and went in the house of study before me, obviously not only here in Tiberias, for there were such houses in different parts of Palestine. When I was just a little girl I used to go there with my father, Rabbi Hanina ben Teradion. That was just fine until the time came when I had to help with the housework. You see, our family was also shaped by patriarchal structures: my brothers didn't have to lift a hand at home, and they could go to the house of study instead. They worked during the day, and in the evening they went to join the discussion. And I? Well, the nights are long, and then I had time to study. But that situation quickly changed, for one day my father heard a discussion between me and my brothers about the interpretation of a passage in the Torah, and he decided that I should be freed from the work at home on some evenings so that I could go with them to the house of study. Because my father taught his children to read the Torah at an early age, my knowledge was superior to that of many older people. During the Bar-Kochba war my father was executed, along with other famous scholars, and my mother and brothers also suffered violent deaths. My sister was carried off to a Roman city. I fled and settled in Tiberias."

"Did you meet your husband, Rabbi Meir, here?"

"Yes, he fled the country during the Bar-Kochba revolt and only returned when Hadrian's anti-Jewish laws were repealed. But Jerusalem was a forbidden city, so he went to Usha. Because he had problems with the patriarchs there he moved to Tiberias and founded his own house of study, which I attended."

"And what happened when you married? Your husband, Rabbi Meir, is a famous scholar. Did he even let you out of the house?—or, to put it another way, could he stand having a woman learned in the Torah by his side?"

Beruriah smiled a little when she heard my question, and then said thoughtfully: "I think that even if he had been against it, *I* would not have let him stop me. But for my husband, knowing the Torah is the most important thing in life, for any human being. How could he forbid me to learn and to teach? Besides, he got to know me through discussions of *halakhah,* and he knew that study of the Torah is my very life."

"Your husband can really be proud to have a brilliant woman like you by his side, one who is even mentioned as a model in the Talmud. It says there that Rabbi Simlai came to Rabbi Jochanan and asked him to teach him the book of the genealogies in three months. Then Rabbi Jochanan said: 'Beruriah, the wife of Rabbi Meir and daughter of Rabbi Hanina ben Teradion, who learned three hundred times three hundred myriads in a single day, could not learn it all in three years, and you are talking about three months?' (*b. Pessachim* 62b)."

She smiled and was silent. After a little while she said: "If my memory serves me, you need to learn the difference between what the Talmud, the Tosefta, and the Mishna say, and what really happened."

"Is what the writings say not true, then?"

"There is no way of representing *the* truth or *the* real. The discussions were handed down orally before they were written down, and what in the end was written was decided by those who were living at the different times when the sayings were collected. They represented *their* truth, and some of what was handed down did not entirely correspond to history. How else would there have been discussions about the Temple at a time when it had long since been destroyed?"

"Oh, now I understand why there are different accounts in the writings. For example, in the Tosefta, in the tractate *Kelim,* Baba Metzia 1.6, you are quoted by name and even supported by an authoritative sage, Rabbi Joshua. The Mishna cites the passage in its tractate *Kelim,* 11.4, but does not mention you."

"That is unfortunately an example of what I was trying to explain to you."

"I have another question. Please don't misunderstand me, but in one place you support the men's judgment concerning women. You are supposed to have met Rabbi Jose, who asked you: 'Which way to Lod?' and you answered: 'Stupid Galilean! The sages said that one should not speak much with a woman; you should have asked: "Which to Lod?"' (*b. Eruwin* 53b–54a). Did you really say that?"

Beruriah laughed aloud. "Do you know, I've often been asked that question. Do you seriously believe that I could really have said such a stupid thing about women?"

"But why is it there?"

"That was also brought about by redaction. Many of those rabbis were men, after all, and they had little interest in seeing that women should have the same rights as they."

"You speak as if that only happened later, and you had a different experience."

"That is not true. I also sense this conflict: that men waver back and forth between what they experience of women around them and what they are accustomed to think about women in a patriarchal society. And in spite of it all, they accept me. The fact that the rabbis' fear of too-wise women—for I can't really call it anything else—has crept into the Talmud suggests that they were acquainted with women who behaved differently."

"So you think that there were other women who studied Torah?" I am truly amazed.

"Of course, why not? Do you think I am the only one? I was just lucky enough to be mentioned in the writings."

"Don't make yourself out to be less than you are! You not only studied Torah, but were also a prominent teacher of the Law!"

"But I am not called 'Rabbi' in the Talmud!"

"Are there other women here in Tiberias who studied Torah?"

"Yes, although not as many as the men. Besides, they seek out opportunities other than the house of study. Most of those who come here are members of rabbinic families."

"What are the other opportunities you mention?"

"Either in our own houses, or in the synagogue, which for us is a gathering place not solely for worship services. Here, incidentally, women also hold leadership roles that you most likely do not suppose we had in antiquity. There are women who are heads of synagogues, elders, or presiders."

"I read in a book about a group of women who devoted their entire lives to the study of the Torah. I think it was Philo of Alexandria who wrote in his book *On the Contemplative Life* about the Therapeutrides, who lived as celibates in double monasteries with their brothers in the faith. It seems that they were mainly to be found in Egypt, but he mentions some in other, non-Greek countries. Do you know anything about them?"

"It could well be that there were, or are, such groups here in Palestine—why not, in a place where so many different social and political movements and groups of people exist? But we do not live in a world like yours, where everything is linked with everything else. Although we hear a lot of things by word of mouth, it may be months or years after the event."

"And what do the rabbis say about women living together in monasteries and studying Torah?"

"What should they say? First of all, they are not omnipotent; they do not prescribe and evaluate everything that takes place in Palestine.

They are teachers of Torah in particular places and schools. Second, their interest is interpreting the Torah, that is, reflecting on how daily life is to be lived, and not what ways of life should be forbidden. No, really, what kind of ideas do you have about the rabbis, since I have to keep emphasizing that *the* rabbis do not exist?"

"What is so special about your teaching that caused you to be included in the Talmud? This is what I have read about you: when a student was muttering over the text, you gave him a kick and said: 'It says, "it is ordered in all things and secure" [2 Sam 23:5]; if [this teaching] is ordered in your 248 members, it is secure for you, but if not, then it is not secure.' (*b. Eruwin* 53b-54a). Is this a special, wholistic kind of understanding of the Torah that was special to you?"

"Oh well, a single saying, and you want to deduce something unique from it."

"Well, yes, but otherwise it wouldn't have been written down, would it?"

"We have already talked long enough about the writing down of sayings. I think this rule may serve to focus once again something that has characterized our religion for centuries, but is repeatedly forgotten: that the Torah must be learned *and* done; it must encompass the entire person. Just look at the Torah psalms. In Ps 19:7-8 we read, 'The law of the LORD is perfect, reviving the soul . . . the precepts of the LORD are right, rejoicing the heart; the commandment of the LORD is clear, enlightening the eyes.' And in Ps 119:103-105 it says, 'How sweet are your words to my taste, sweeter than honey to my mouth! Through your precepts I get understanding. . . . Your word is a lamp to my feet and light to my path.' Again and again we find descriptions of how these precepts affect all parts of the body, and that the Torah is to be praised and acclaimed with a loud voice. So what is new about my understanding of the Torah? I am only trying to live and teach the tradition."

"You are quite right, but the Torah can be interpreted very differently. So you made a rule: 'Pay attention to the end of the verse.' What did you mean by that?"

"I can explain that to you by means of an example. There were some ruffians who lived near my husband; they bullied him, and Meir prayed that they would die. Then I said: 'You are relying on the verse, "Let sinners be consumed from the earth" (Ps 104:35). But in fact it says "sins," not "sinners." And consider the end of the verse: "and let the wicked be no more." If sin is destroyed, there will be no more sinners left. You should instead pray for mercy for them, so that they may do penance.' So he asked for mercy for them, and they did penance" (*b. Berakhot* 10a).

"Now I would like to ask *you* a question. Some of you twentieth-century feminists seem to think that our era was especially patriarchal, and that yours is free of it. Is that so? I mean, quite a few centuries have passed, so it would not be surprising."

What was I supposed to answer? She was right to ask me that. Now it was up to me to talk about our century. "You know, as far as women's social position is concerned some things have changed, and even improved. But we are still a long way from being equal to men. I can tell you a little about the German Christian context, especially the field of theological teaching: Theology is a field of scholarship that for a very long time was reserved to the world of men. It only opened to women in the beginning of the twentieth century. That was a subject for rejoicing, of course, but as so often happens, there was a catch: passing the examinations in theology did not guarantee women employment in the churches or in theology. Instead, they could only do diaconal and educational work, primarily as teachers. A few years later, under pressure from young women theologians, women were also made vicars or deaconesses, but again they were not accorded a status equal to that of their male colleagues. They were restricted to certain sectors of pastoral work in congregations: work with women, children, and young people, teaching and pastoral care, but not presiding at the sacraments or congregational leadership. Like the teachers, they had to make promises of celibacy; that is, if they married they had to resign their offices. What was especially unfair was that they were not ordained, but only blessed."

Beruriah had listened with fascination; now she interrupted: "But that is not equality of men and women. For them to have to give up their profession because they married is unheard-of. But in the period in which you are living this rule no longer applies, right?"

"No, but it was in force until 1969! And I am living in the year 1998. Up to the late 1960s, women who wanted to continue careers as theologians had to look for other means. A few got into the universities that way—a lucky break for some, wouldn't you say? Our generation can learn a lot from women like Luise Schottroff, the professor with whom I studied. But those few women didn't have an easy time of it, especially when they didn't go along with the generally accepted opinions, but took a critical position."

Beruriah nodded understandingly. "Oh, yes, I can sing that tune myself. As a matter of fact, I live in a tradition that needs controversy and discussion about the meaning of the Torah. But when *I* say something it gets turned over not just once, but twice and sometimes even three times. In spite of it all, students come to me to enter discussions and learn from me. I also find it interesting, in your account, that women were allowed to teach children and young people."

"Why? For one thing, the younger generation don't yet possess the status of grownups; and second, child care and pedagogical work are seen as something 'innate' to women. You can also see this in the fact that at the beginning of the twentieth century there were hardly any women to be found teaching in the upper schools. That, at least, has changed in the course of the century."

"But you can accomplish the most with young people, and it is also easiest to 'go wrong' with them. What people learn in their childhood they will never forget: it shapes them!"

"You are saying something that I have often thought, but have the gentlemen of the theological cadre considered it? It is so obvious in my own context that in our modern society the teachers of religion influence the religious character of the people if anyone does at all. After all, who in our time is still brought up as a Christian at home, or grows up in a Christian community? In my country Christians can still feel lucky that religious instruction is protected in the constitution."

"Are you telling me that religion is no longer a part of your life? You need laws to insure that the message of the liberating God reaches people?"

"You can say that. From that point of view you live in a different world."

In the days that followed I remained in Tiberias to get acquainted with that "different world." Through Beruriah I met a great many women who did not fit my picture of *the* woman in Judaism. Their very conditions of life disallowed generalizations about them. But Beruriah taught me once again that there were women in history who sought their own way in the patriarchal world and were recognized for it, even though their lives were certainly not easy!

Bibliography

The Babylonian Talmud. Translated into English with notes, glossary, and indices under the editorship of Isidore Epstein. 7 parts in 18 vols. London: Soncino, 1961.

Ben-Sasson, Chaim Hillel, ed. *Geschichte des jüdischen Volkes. Von den Anfängen bis zur Gegenwart.* Munich: Beck, 1992.

Brooten, Bernadette J. "Jüdinnen zur Zeit Jesu. Ein Plädoyer für Differenzierung," in Bernadette J. Brooten and Norbert Greinacher, eds., *Frauen in der Männerkirche*. Munich and Mainz: Kaiser, 1982, 141–48.

Cunow, Dietlinde. "'Im Falle einer Eheschließung endet das Dienstverhältnis.' Rückblick auf die Zölibatsklausel bei Pastorinnen," in Frauenforschungsprojekt zur Geschichte der Theologinnen Göttingen, eds., *Querdenken. Beiträge zur feministisch-befreiungstheologischen Diskussion*. Festschrift für Hannelore Erhart zum 65. Geburtstag. 2nd ed. Pfaffenweiler: Centaurus, 1993, 307–09.

Erhart, Hannelore. "Der lange Weg der Theologinnen ins Amt," in Dorothee Sölle, ed., *Für Gerechtigkeit streiten. Theologie im Alltag einer bedrohten Welt*. Gütersloh: Chr. Kaiser, 1994, 137–44.

Henze, Dagmar, Claudia Janssen, Stefanie Müller, and Beate Wehn. *Antijudaismus im Neuen Testament? Grundlagen für die Arbeit mit biblischen Texten*. Gütersloh: Chr. Kaiser, 1997.

Ilan, Tal. *Mine and Yours Are Hers. Retrieving Women's History from Rabbinic Literature*. Leiden: Brill, 1997.

Levinson, Pnina Navè. *Was wurde aus Saras Töchtern? Frauen im Judentum*. 2nd ed. Gütersloh: Gerd Mohn, 1990.

Neusner, Jacob. *The Talmud: Introduction and Reader*. Atlanta: Scholars, 1995.

The Talmud of Babylonia: An American Translation. Translated by Jacob Neusner. Brown Judaic Studies 63– . Chico, Calif., and Atlanta: Scholars, 1984– .

Beate Wehn

"I Am a Handmaid of the Living God!"
The Apostle Thecla and the
Consequences of Transgression

Beyond the canonical limits of the New Testament, in the early Christian Apostolic Acts from the second and third centuries, we encounter the story of the deeds of the apostle Thecla (= *AT*). A feminist-socio-historical investigation of this story is a venturesome undertaking: Just as we may often find traces of an older painting hidden beneath the surface of a later one, so the story of Thecla, behind the often transfigured image of the martyr and saint, provides us with glimpses of the life of an early Christian itinerant apostle. The picture that emerges is that of a transgressive woman, treading between Hellenistic-Roman society and early Christian community. Thecla's path repeatedly transgresses boundaries: she abandons familiar people, social structures, and places; she disappoints the role expectations of her family of origin and—against Paul's wishes, too—confidently goes her own way. In doing so she experiences betrayal, abandonment, and homelessness, violence and the fear of death, but also the concern and aid of strangers, and joyful community in the houses of her fellow believers—as well as the saving intervention of God, of which she boldly sings.

In an attempt to discover the living woman Thecla beneath the "lacquer" of the heroine, martyr, and saint, and below the surface of primarily androcentric interpretations, we cannot avoid focusing our attention on Thecla and Paul's encounter with Alexander in Antioch: a meeting that hints at the danger and struggle that awaited transgressive women in early Christianity, and that also dis-closes our usual view of Paul. It is this part of Thecla's story that I want to examine here.

19

"I will follow you wherever you go!" Thecla's Breakthrough

Thecla's story begins with Paul's arrival in her home town of Iconium. While the itinerant apostle is preaching in the house of Onesiphorus, Thecla sits at the window of the house next door and listens with fascination, "night and day" (7).[1] Paul's preaching about continence, that is, a life without marriage, and about the resurrection leads Thecla to faith in the God whom Paul preaches. Her relatives are concerned about this development. Her mother, Theocleia, and Thecla's fiancé Thamyris worry about the order in their own and Thecla's lives if Thecla is serious about remaining unmarried, so that the pairing of the betrothed couple, both of them from prominent families, will not take place. As a result, Thamyris brings Paul before the city governor and accuses him: "Thou hast destroyed the city of the Iconians, and my betrothed, so that she will not have me . . ." (15). Paul is put on trial and imprisoned. After this Thecla bribes the prison guards every night and so gets in to see Paul. She "sat at his feet and heard about the mighty deeds of God" (18). Thecla appears here as Paul's courageous disciple and knowledge-hungry student. Her family looks for her and finds her with Paul. Now both of them are brought before the judgment seat. Thecla's trial centers on the question whether she will marry Thamyris, as is the custom in Iconium. When she does not answer, but gazes at Paul like one hypnotized, her mother demands that Thecla be burned, "that all the women who have been taught by this man may be afraid" (20). The governor then has Paul exiled from the city and sentences Thecla to be burned. Her fate seems to be sealed when she stands naked on the pyre in the amphitheatre. She forms a cross with her body, thus associating her suffering with the cross of Christ. Through the mercy of God, Thecla is saved: the fire does not touch her and a sudden rainstorm puts out the flames.

After her rescue Thecla goes in search of Paul and finally finds him in an open cave tomb on the road to Daphne. Here Paul, Onesiphorus, Lectra, and their children have been fasting and praying for Thecla's rescue. Their joy is profound:

> And within the tomb there was much love, Paul rejoicing, and Onesiphorus and all of them. But they had five loaves, and vegetables, and water, and they were joyful over the holy works of

[1] All quotations from the Acts of Thecla are taken from Edgar Hennecke and Wilhelm Schneemelcher, eds., *New Testament Apocrypha*. English translation supervised by Robert McL. Wilson (2nd rev. ed. Louisville: Westminster/John Knox, 1992) 2:239–46.

Christ. And Thecla said to Paul: "I will cut my hair short and follow thee wherever thou goest." But he said: "The season is unfavourable, and thou art comely. May no other temptation come upon thee, worse than the first, and thou endure not and play the coward!" And Thecla said: "Only give me the seal in Christ, and temptation shall not touch me." And Paul said: "Have patience, Thecla, and thou shalt receive the water." (*AT* 25)

Here Paul refuses to baptize Thecla. Later, while fighting the wild beasts in Antioch, Thecla will baptize herself in face of death. Now comes the scene that is the focus of our inquiry. Thecla has apparently prevailed in her determination to follow Paul:

> And Paul sent away Onesiphorus with all his family to Iconium, and so taking Thecla came into Antioch. But immediately as they entered a Syrian by the name of Alexander, one of the first of the Antiochenes, seeing Thecla fell in love with her, and sought to win over Paul with money and gifts. But Paul said: "I do not know the woman of whom thou dost speak, nor is she mine." But he [Alexander], being a powerful man, embraced her on the open street; she however would not endure it, but looked about for Paul and cried out bitterly, saying: "Force not the stranger, force not the handmaid of God! Among the Iconians I am one of the first, and because I did not wish to marry Thamyris I have been cast out of the city." And taking hold of Alexander she ripped his cloak, took off the crown from his head, and made him a laughingstock. But he, partly out of love for her and partly in shame at what had befallen him, brought her before the governor; and when she confessed that she had done these things, he condemned her to the beasts. (*AT* 26-27)

The encounter between Alexander, Thecla, and Paul in Antioch has preserved only a shadowy existence in the history of interpretation, perhaps because this is a key passage in the critique of Paul represented by the Acts of Thecla. Among the few interpreters who have given close attention to Paul's role in Antioch, Luise Schottroff (1993) has expressed the sharpest criticism of his behavior. Let us now consider this apparently shocking scene in the Acts of Thecla in the narrower context of ancient Roman law.

Banished from Iconium, Threatened in Antioch: Thecla as Doubly Foreign

In *AT* 26 we find Thecla journeying with Paul, much like Prisca and Aquila, Junia and Andronicus in the New Testament. In early Christianity it was not unusual for missionaries, whether married or unmarried, to travel together, but they may have seemed shocking to Hellenistic-Roman society. They did not fit within the established order of the sexes with which Thecla had just broken. As she arrives in Antioch she is aware of what can happen to a young woman who, out of her newly-acquired faith-conviction, chooses to remain unmarried and to travel with an apostle. (For the question of celibacy see Luzia Sutter-Rehmann, 1994.) She has left her previous social, religious, and economic ties and security behind (cf. Musurillo 1972, 281). And she has experienced in her own body how little understanding her relatives have for her new way of life, when she was displayed naked to be burned in the arena "that all the women who have been taught by this man [Paul] may be afraid" (20). Women who step out of the (sex-)roles prescribed for them are evidently regarded as a serious threat to the patriarchal order of society. Thecla is to be made an example, so that other women who might otherwise follow her example may be intimidated and domesticated (cf. the story of Vashti in the book of Esther).

In the apocryphal literature we often read that women who came to believe in Christ changed their outward appearance, their hair and their clothing, as an expression of their new self-concept, one that broke with the ideals of their social environment (for hair, cf. the *Acts of Thomas* 114; a linen garment, ibid. 121). So it seems that Thecla also, on her arrival in Antioch, cut her hair and perhaps wore simpler garments than she had previously donned. It is said of Thecla that, after being rescued from the beasts, she "sewed her mantle into a cloak after the fashion of men"—that is, she shortened it (*AT* 40)—before setting out on her journey to Myra.

In Antioch, Thecla was apparently mistaken by Alexander, a leading man in the city, for a woman at the disposal of her companion. Hence Alexander first attempts to gain possession of Thecla through Paul, having, according to the text, "fallen in love" with her. Behind Alexander's supposition lies the ancient Roman law whereby men had the power to dispose of the women belonging to them: daughters were under the authority of their fathers, wives under that of their husbands, prostitutes under that of their pimps, etc. The text does not tell us what kind of relationship Alexander presumes existed between Thecla and Paul: did he think she was Paul's daughter, or a prostitute accompanying her pimp? In any case, what is important is Paul's response: "I do not know the woman of whom thou dost speak [that is: I have no close relationship with her]; nor is she mine." Paul distances himself from Thecla by making clear that he has no authority over her, which is true as far as the legal situation is concerned. But in this situation it has dramatic consequences for Thecla, for as a (beautiful) woman and a stranger in the city, bereft of the protection of male relatives, she is completely vulnerable to the lust of Alexander and other men. The fact that Thecla is left alone, at the mercy of Alexander, is shown by her looking around for Paul as Alexander embraces her in the open street. This is the beginning, for Thecla, of a violent sequence that once again brings her to the brink of death.

A Violent Man Accuses His Victim—and Wins

The narrative tells us that Alexander embraced Thecla because he was a powerful man. Did Roman law really permit liberties of that kind? How else could it happen that not the perpetrator, but his victim was condemned by the governor? We need to pursue this question. In ancient Roman law the definition of a crime included both the *iniuria* (criminal action, wrong done) and the *stuprum per vim* (damage, etc.) involved in a violent act such as that suffered by Thecla. *Iniuria* is injury to a person "either in the person or in his or her rights or honor" (Mommsen 1982, 787). Among the cases that involve *iniuria* were "every action damaging to the honor of a respectable woman" (Mommsen 1982, 792), including "offensive encounters on public streets, lewd public address, removal of the person accompanying her" (ibid.). The mere attempt to do such a thing was punishable. Beginning with the first century of the Common Era, the woman who suffered the *iniuria* could bring an accusation herself (cf. Stahlmann 1997, 55). But Roman law divided women into two classes: honorable, free Roman women were contrasted with "dishonorable" women, including slaves and prostitutes. The latter were regarded as suspicious before the law, and the law in turn was not applied equally to them. The two groups were supposed to be distinguishable by their clothing. This Augustan law was meant to effect both the public protection and the disciplining of free Roman women. This two-class set of rights had real significance for the person accused of *iniuria*: "If someone accosts a virgin (with an obvious intent), provided she is wearing a slave's gown, it appears that he is less guilty; and he is still less guilty if she is dressed like a prostitute and not like a *mater familias*. Thus if the woman is not wearing the customary dress of a *matrona* and someone accosts her or removes her escort he is to be accused of a personal injury [= *iniuria*]" (Ulpian, *Dig.* 47.10.15.15; quoted from Stahlmann 1997, 57).

Near the beginning of the second century Papian defines *stuprum* as "immorality . . . with a virgin or widow" (*Dig.* 48.5.6.1; cf. Mod. *Dig.* 48.5.35). *Stuprum* could occur with or without the application of force; in the latter case the law speaks of *per vim stuprum*, meaning rape. According to the legal provisions the victim of a rape was not subject to social degradation; that is, she was regarded by the law as clearly the victim of a capital offense against public order (cf. Stahlmann 1997, 65ff.). The raped woman could make the accusation herself, as could her father or husband. In judgments on the severity of *per vim stuprum* the honorable or dishonorable character of the victim played no part: "This clearly shows that this Julian law was about the disciplining of men, not of women" (Stahlmann 1997, 66).

Alexander's attack on Thecla can be understood in terms of the crimes of *iniuria* and *per vim stuprum,* even if Thecla was already expressing her new way of life through a changed outward appearance, so that she could not be seen at first glance to be a free Roman woman. According to the law Alexander both offends her dignity *(iniuria)* and applies force *(per vim stuprum)* to achieve his end. Under the Roman law then in effect he could have been accused by Thecla, but instead Alexander, using his position of power, in no time at all makes the innocent victim the accused: "Although we later discover that Thecla is said to be 'guilty of sacrilege,' the narrator has made it clear that such a charge would never have been levied against her if she had submitted to Alexander's desire. This implies that, in the storyteller's view, the rejection of Roman authority and a woman's refusal of sexual activity are functionally equivalent and need not be distinguished" (McGinn 1994, 816).

And Paul? Dis-couraging Revelations in Thecla's Story

Paul distances himself from Thecla by making it clear that he has no authority over her. Then he disappears from the scene, for Thecla seeks him in vain while she is in danger. How should we understand Paul's behavior in the context of Thecla's story?

It is possible that the story of Abraham's surrender of Sarah (Gen 12:10-20), which is echoed here, may give us an indication of Paul's motive for denying Thecla: "The couple leaves their land and goes to Egypt to escape famine. When they reach the border, Abram loses his nerve. He fears that the Egyptians are sexual libertines and might kill him in order to get at his beautiful wife. He tries to talk Sarai into going along with his plan by telling people she is his sister" (Fischer 1998, 13). Abraham does this solely in his own interest, out of fear of what he supposes to be the helplessness and dearth of rights of foreigners. To save his own life he sacrifices Sarah (cf. also Gen 20:1-18; 26:1-11).

Paul and Thecla arrive in Antioch as foreigners in transit. They are not foreigners in the Roman empire, but there is danger for people who are strangers in any particular place if they appear suspect to the Roman authorities, or if they are accused because of their religious practices (cf. Acts 16:16-24), as had already happened to Paul in Iconium. Was Paul afraid that he would be imprisoned because of his beautiful companion? Did he fear a latent threat from the powerful people of the locality? Did he run away out of fear of imprisonment or even death? The text leaves the reasons for his action open; the only thing certain is that he abandons Thecla when he should have been protecting her.

Roman law emphasized the importance of a woman's escort: whoever removed such an escort could be punished, because he would bring the woman into a dangerous situation like the one in which Paul left Thecla. This penal rule apparently responded to a social reality: unescorted women were subject to a latent threat of attack by strange men. Thus what Thecla experienced in Antioch may not have appeared strange to her contemporaries.

Paul's behavior toward Thecla is inexcusable, though we must not lose sight of the fact that Alexander was the actual attacker. Paul becomes an accomplice in the crime because he must have known what the consequences of his action would be for Thecla. Nevertheless, Alexander's actions against Thecla because of her resistance (*AT* 27-35) show that Paul's probable fears in this situation were fundamentally justified: influence and power suddenly turn victims into accused criminals.

In *AT* 26 and the preceding encounter in *AT* 25 the critical depiction of Paul that pervades the story of Thecla reaches its climax. While Thecla from the beginning has an emotional attachment to Paul and stubbornly follows him, Paul is shown as being at least ambivalent in his attitude to Thecla. When they meet again after Thecla has been rescued from a fiery death in Iconium Paul is joyful, but he refuses to baptize her because he apparently doubts her faith and her ability to persevere—as if the pyre had not been a serious "testing" (cf. McGinn 1994, 816).

In referring here to Thecla's beauty Paul also reveals that, just like Alexander, he regards Thecla first of all as a lovely woman, and imagines that she is susceptible to male attempts at seduction. Ultimately, however, it is not Thecla who surrenders her faith in Christ, which she also expresses through her continent way of life. Instead, Paul betrays his companion at the very moment when her bodily integrity and her religious identity are threatened. In Iconium Paul had preached: "Blessed are they who have kept the flesh pure, for they shall become a temple of God . . . . Blessed are the bodies of the virgins, for they shall be well pleasing to God, and shall not lose the reward of their purity . . ." (*AT* 5-6). Should not Paul be measured against these words? As a member of Thecla's "new family," her teacher and companion in Antioch, is he not obligated to stand by Thecla as she resists Alexander, and to protect her body, which is a temple of God?

Female Resistance and Injured Male Pride:
An Old Story

Thecla defends herself desperately and with all her strength against Alexander's attempt to take possession of her. In the struggle his robe and wreath, status symbols in ancient society, are damaged. Alexander himself becomes an object of mirth and is ashamed at having such a thing happen to him. His next actions can be understood in light of the observation that (attempted) rape had a social and political dimension in ancient society: "It rested on the idea that beautiful women, as valuable property, belonged of right to the powerful and respectable men, and an acknowledgment of this underscored their position" (Doblhofer 1994, 44). From the point of view of the man himself "rape of beautiful victims was an expression and intensification of his claim to a leading role" (ibid.). By defending herself against this sexual attack Thecla called Alexander's power and claims to leadership into question. He saw his social reputation wounded by the public scandal that Thecla's resistance created for him. He could not allow such shame to remain upon him. The parallels between Thamyris, Thecla's former fiancé, and Alexander are obvious: Both say that they love Thecla, but for the sake of their own public reputations they could not tolerate Thecla's resistance. Their supposed love for Thecla is ultimately revealed as a claim to possession and power over her. This also explains why their "love" was so rapidly turned into an action whose consequences threatened Thecla's very life.

In Iconium Thecla had been handed over to be burned because she refused to marry Thamyris, and preferred to live unmarried. In Antioch, brought before the governor because of her resistance to Alexander, she is to be killed by beasts in the arena. For Thecla the assumption of a role not in accord with the social norm for women and resistance to being seized and made the property of a strange man are actions to be punished by death. As a consequence of Alexander's wounded pride, his power, and his influence, Thecla, although it is she who is the victim of violence, once again finds herself before the judgment seat.

There are striking parallels to these power structures in Antioch in the story of Susanna in the additions to the book of Daniel. Susanna, a Jewish woman, is made the victim of an attempted rape in her husband's garden by two elders and judges of the town. Susanna at first successfully defends herself against them, but out of rage and injured pride these elder-judges bring a public accusation against her and put her on trial. In order to bring about Susanna's death they accuse her of adultery with an unknown man. During the trial they strip Susanna and lay their hands on her head, thus continuing in a public forum the violence they began in the garden. The elder-judges' calculation almost succeeds: the crowd believes them, and Susanna is condemned to die. She is already on the way to execution when a young man named Daniel questions the validity of the trial and exposes the judges' statements as lies. Susanna escapes death, and it falls instead on the elder-judges.

Susanna's and Thecla's experiences reveal some obvious similarities: their resistance to (sexual) violence is followed by the revenge of their attackers, who use their positions of power to bring their victims before the court and accuse them of a capital crime. Just as Susanna undergoes a continuation of (sexual) violence as she stands before the judicial bench, so Thecla must undergo the same thing as she is led through the town and brought into the amphitheatre. Susanna and Thecla are described as victims and yet as active women who know that God is on their side, even in hopeless situations. God's intervention and the aid of human beings ultimately rescue them from death.

Escaped from Death:
Thecla as Apostle and Teacher

Before her struggle with the beasts Thecla is welcomed by Tryphaena, a rich widow whose dead daughter Falconilla appears to her in a dream and begs her to take to herself "the stranger, the desolate Thecla" (*AT* 28) in her stead. Tryphaena does so and protects Thecla against possible rape by the governor's soldiers. Even on the day she is delivered to the beasts Tryphaena does not abandon Thecla to Alexander and the soldiers, but despairingly brings her in person to the place where she is to encounter the animals. Thecla is rescued from the beasts through a miraculous sequence of events, in the course of which she baptizes herself, and she answers the governor, when he wonders why none of the beasts touched her:

> I am a handmaid of the living God. . . . I have believed in him in whom God is well pleased, His Son. For his sake not one of the beasts touched me. For he alone is the goal of salvation and the foundation of immortal life. To the storm-tossed he is a refuge, to the oppressed relief, to the despairing shelter; in a word, whoever does not believe in him shall not live, but die for ever. (*AT* 37)

After this impressive confession Thecla is released by the governor; she remains some days longer with Tryphaena, "instructing her in the word of God, so that the majority of the maidservants also believed; and there was great joy in the house" (*AT* 39). When Thecla leaves that house to go to find Paul she leaves behind her a house church. In Myra she finds Paul and tells him what has happened, and that she has baptized herself in the name of God and now intends to go to Iconium. Paul's commission, "Go and teach the word of God!" only confirms Thecla's existing apostolic praxis, already begun in Antioch. On her return to Iconium, Thecla seeks out the place where her story began, the house of Onesiphorus. Once again she makes a profession of faith that reflects her internal relationship with God:

> My God, and God of this house where the light shone upon me, Christ Jesus the Son of God, my helper in prison, my helper before governors, my helper in the fire, my helper among the beasts, thou art God, and to thee be the glory for ever. Amen. (*AT* 42)

Thecla's story ends in Seleucia, where she dies after having worked a long time as an apostle.

"Certain Women" and Other Annoyances

The Acts of Thecla was a well-known and highly esteemed document in the early centuries of Christianity (cf. Jensen 1998, 742); in recent times some writers have attributed its authorship to women as well (e.g., Davies 1980). In any case it seems certain that it originated in and was handed down by groups of early Christian women (Burrus 1987; MacDonald 1984). In light of the ambivalent and even critical depiction of Paul in the Thecla story this last seems to me assured: here we find a reflection of the experiences and conflicts of early Christian women with their brothers in the faith and in their non-Christian social world.

A statement by the Church father Tertullian is revealing as regards the history of the impact of Thecla's story: "When certain women appeal to that wrongly entitled writing [*The Acts of Paul*] (and) the example of Thecla in defense of women's right to teach and to baptize, they should know that in Asia the presbyter who wrote that document and in this way attributed his own (inventions) to Paul, alleged that he had done it out of love for Paul, and he was removed from his office" (Tertullian, *De Baptismo* 17.4; quoted in Jensen 1995, 72).

Tertullian's statement shows that there were many women who followed Thecla's example by teaching, baptizing, and pursuing a celibate way of life. It also suggests that the critique of Paul expressed in the story of Thecla was known to the early Church fathers, who were annoyed by it. Tertullian continues by pointing to the injunction for women to keep silence in 1 Cor 14:34-35, as a support for his argument. In doing so he uses only Paul's misogynistic sayings, and no doubt there are some. But at the same time we may not overlook the fact that the same Paul speaks admiringly and with veneration of the women who worked with him in mission and regards them as equal colleagues (cf. Rom 16:1-16; Schottroff 1993, 13–14).

The story of Thecla is very important for the reconstruction of the lives of early Christian women, when it is placed in dialogue with New Testament texts describing women's preaching and teaching. Canonical and apocryphal texts shed light on one another. The same is true for the (feminist) study of the Pauline tradition: the story of Thecla presents an ambivalent picture of Paul and directs a clear critique at his behavior. The fact that this critique, inherent in the narrative, has scarcely been recognized in the past gives rise to the question whether the story of Thecla here comes up against a theological taboo: is it not permissible that there should be such a Paul as the one here described?

I have referred to the depiction of Paul in the story of Thecla as "disappointing." A rent is opened in the traditional image of Paul, and it should be taken seriously, for it shows Paul, the apostle and the man, in the light in which he appeared to the women and men who handed down the story of Thecla: as one who was complicit in the violence perpetrated against Thecla. Nevertheless, this memory of Paul, heretofore obviously dangerous, could be a healing memory if we seize the opportunity to rediscover the apostle—from the critical perspective of the story of Thecla.

As far as Thecla is concerned, it is time at last to take seriously her experiences with violence and public torture, and to call them what they are. When we look more closely we find gaps in her story that raise disturbing questions: why does Thecla repeatedly return to Paul, even though he leaves her in the lurch? How does she deal with the violence done to her? We cannot ask Thecla. But we can listen to the women today who are survivors of violence. They may be able to fill in the gaps in Thecla's story with their experiences of violence, their pain, their accusations, and their strength to survive.

Bibliography

Burrus, Virginia. *Chastity as Autonomy. Women in the Stories of the Apocryphal Acts.* Lewiston, N.Y., and Queenston, Ontario: Edwin Mellen, 1987.

Castelli, Elizabeth. "Virginity and Its Meaning for Women's Sexuality in Early Christianity," *JFSR* 2 (1986) 61–88.

Davies, Stevan L. *The Revolt of the Widows. The Social World of the Apocryphal Acts.* Carbondale: Southern Illinois University Press, 1980.

Doblhofer, Georg. *Vergewaltigung in der Antike.* Stuttgart: B. G. Teubner, 1994.

Fischer, Irmtraud. "Genesis 12–50. Die Ursprungsgeschichte Israels als Frauen-geschichte," in Luise Schottroff and Marie-Therese Wacker, eds., *Kompendium Feministische Bibelauslegung.* Gütersloh: Chr.Kaiser/Gütersloher Verlagshaus, 1998, 12–25.

Hennecke, Edgar, and Wilhelm Schneemelcher, eds., *New Testament Apocrypha.* English translation supervised by Robert McL. Wilson. 2nd rev. ed. Louisville: Westminster/John Knox, 1992, 2:239–46.

Jensen, Anne. *Thekla – die Apostolin. Ein apokrypher Text neu entdeckt.* Translated and commented by Anne Jensen. Freiburg, Basel, and Vienna: Herder, 1995.

_____. "Die Theklageschichte. Die Apostolin zwischen Fiktionalität und Realität," in Luise Schottroff and Marie-Therese Wacker, eds., *Kompendium Feministische Bibelauslegung.* Gütersloh: Chr.Kaiser/Gütersloher Verlagshaus, 1998, 742–47.

MacDonald, Dennis R. "The Role of Women in the Production of the Apocryphal Acts of Apostles," *Iliff Review* 40/4 (1984) 21–38.

McGinn, Sheila E. "The Acts of Thecla," in Elisabeth Schüssler Fiorenza, ed., *Searching the Scriptures.* New York: Crossroad, 1994, 2:800–28.

Mommsen, Theodor. *Römisches Strafrecht.* Leipzig: Duncker & Humblot, 1899; Munich: Beck, 1982.

Musurillo, Herbert, ed. *The Acts of the Christian Martyrs.* Oxford: Clarendon Press, 1972.

Schottroff, Luise. "'Ich kenne die Frau nicht . . . sie ist auch nicht mein.' Die zwei Gesichter des Paulus," in Renate Jost and Ursula Kubera, eds., *Wie Theologen Frauen sehen—von der Macht der Bilder.* Freiburg, Basel, and Vienna: Herder, 1993.

_____. "Frauengeschrei. Frauenwiderstand und Frauensolidarität in den Theklaakten," *Schlangenbrut* 50 (1995) 5–8.

Stahlmann, Ines. *Der gefesselte Sexus. Weibliche Keuschheit und Askese im Westen des Römischen Reiches.* Berlin: Akademie Verlag, 1997.

Sutter Rehmann, Luzia. "'Und ihr werdet ohne Sorge sein . . .' Gedanken zum Phänomen der Ehefreiheit im frühen Christentum," in Dorothee Sölle, ed., *Für Gerechtigkeit streiten. Theologie im Alltag einer bedrohten Welt.* Gütersloh: Chr. Kaiser, 1994, 88–95.

Claudia Janssen

Paul:
Walking the Line between Traditions and Ages

Who is interested in the letters of Paul anymore? Professors, pastors, teachers, maybe a few zealous Mass-goers? Who else? The texts are foreign to quite a few even of those who are studying theology, and their content is strange—although, of course, they are covered on examinations and therefore one has to be somewhat familiar with them! But outside this narrow theological context is there any reason to go on reading Paul's letters? It seems to be interesting, and not only for scholars, to learn more about Jesus, to reflect on his words and actions—as, among other things, the unabated flood of popular books and films indicates. But Paul? Does he have anything left to say to us today, in our postmodern, post-Christian world?

Unlike the figure of Jesus, which, as new light is shed upon it, changes with time and according to personal theological preferences, the person of Paul appears easy to describe with precision. After all, unlike Jesus, Paul has left us letters written with his own hand, and from them we can deduce a great deal about his person, his thoughts, and his life. Before I became acquainted with feminist theological study of Paul I had a pretty clear picture of him in mind: certainly influenced by my Protestant tradition, I pictured Paul as similar to the young Luther on the Wartburg, sitting in his bare room and brooding over important theological questions. The lectures I heard at the university supported that image. While I saw Jesus as an itinerant prophet still bound up in Judaism, always on the move with a large group of people, there was no doubt that Paul was a single individual, the founder of the Christian church. His writings contained theoretical reflections on Jesus' proclamation of the reign of God as a way of life. And while his first letters were still aimed at resolving concrete problems within the communities, the Letter to the Romans constituted the brilliant conclusion and carefully composed theoretical summary of all the theological knowledge he had acquired: the first Christian dogmatics, utterly binding and unsurpassed in its power of expression to the present day.

Paul, the undisputed authority, the patriarch of his churches, which he directed with a firm hand and clear words—with this man, over the centuries, popes, bishops, professors, and even village pastors in congregations could easily identify. Women, on the other hand, were at the bottom of the hierarchy. They were responsible for diaconal work and not for theology; after all, Jesus and Paul were both men! The saying in 1 Cor 14:34: "Let the women keep silent in the churches," has had a fatal history of effectiveness even into our own day; it has led to the circumstance that women have been represented scarcely or not at all in leadership positions in the churches, something that was always quite all right with the men in power—and still is! Paul's authority governs even now, and not only in that instance. For example, when it is a question of permitting lesbian or gay pastors and priests to work in our congregations, Paul's words in Romans, where he speaks of "degrading passions" and "unnatural intercourse" contrary to the will of God the creator (Rom 1:26-27) are used as an argument against them. Homosexual couples do not have Paul's blessing, and hence do not enjoy that of today's churches either.

Who was Paul? What picture develops if we examine his letters while deliberately distancing ourselves from the traditional, authoritarian portrayal of his person and personality?

The historical Paul

In a talk given in 1951 the New Testament scholar Ernst Käsemann posed a central question that still preoccupies feminist research today: Does the New Testament canon offer a basis for church unity? Käsemann is here dealing with one of the central phenomena that confronts historians when they consider the form of the early church: the many voices audible in the tradition. We have four gospels in which we find different and to some extent contradictory descriptions of events. The letters of Paul also witness to a multiplicity of different opinions and conflicts.

Käsemann was criticizing a tradition that overlooks that multiplicity and sees Scripture primarily as a fund of dogmatic assertions. He points to the dialogical character of most New Testament texts: "Exegesis suffers from the fact that we generally perceive the conversation partner or opponent only through the eyes of the speaker, and are thus led astray into one-sided judgments and hasty conclusions" (Käsemann 1986, 89). As examples he mentions some conflicts in which Paul was involved:

"Was Peter able to respond to Paul's accusations at Antioch, and did he agree with him, or did these two enter into public conflict? . . . What was all that about Apollos, to whom the enthusiasts in Corinth seem to have appealed? . . . Who were the envious persons who, at the time when the letter to the Philippians was written, were using Paul's imprisonment against the apostle? How fragile must his authority have been during his own lifetime if anyone could dare to do that!" (ibid.). Käsemann concludes that the New Testament canon must have been far more extensive than what we now have. "But that means that what we have retained in the canon are only scraps of the conversations conducted in early Christianity, and that the variability of the primitive Christian kerygma must have been much greater even than our observation of the situation retained in the canon allows us to see" (ibid. 90).

Käsemann here gives voice to two important observations:

1. Paul's authority was by no means so undisputed as it seems to us today. This is clear not only from the conflicts referred to, but also from a further point: Some of the post-Pauline letters of a later generation rest on his authority and were written in his name (e.g., Ephesians, Colossians, 2 Thessalonians, and the Pastoral Letters 1 and 2 Timothy and Titus), while others do not mention him at all (e.g., the Johannine letters, the first letter of Peter, Hebrews, James). Were they unaware of Paul, or did they deliberately ignore him and his theology?

2. In Paul's letters we always hear his position; the responses have not been handed on to us. Much of what seemed offensive at a later time was certainly and deliberately destroyed or sorted out. The canon that we now have in our New Testament already reflects a part of the history of power in the church of the first centuries. Here we should mention especially the Pastoral Letters which, as purposeful pseudepigrapha written in Paul's name, attempt to condemn women to silence and subordination to their husbands. One important text, the *Acts of Thecla*, in which a woman criticizes Paul's behavior and acts independently as a theologian contrary to his wishes, unlike the Pastoral Letters was not included in the canon, even though it originated at about the same time.

The *Acts of Thecla* and other so-called apocryphal texts are for feminist scholars a rich resource in which they rediscover fragments of early Christian discussions that had been thought lost, and attempt to give voice to these women and men who had been made invisible— always in the awareness that a great deal is in fact irretrievably lost. One short passage from the *Acts of Thecla* constitutes an astonishingly revealing resource for our question about the "historical Paul." A man named Onesiphorus, who has heard that Paul is on his way to Iconium, goes out to meet and welcome him. "And he saw Paul coming, a man small of stature, with a bald head and crooked legs, in a good state of body, with eyebrows meeting and nose somewhat hooked, full of friendliness; for now he appeared like a man, and now he had the face of an angel" (*AT* 2-3).[1]

Our Paul-Lenses

From what has been said it is clear how deeply our ideas about Paul and his time are shaped by material from the tradition. To put it in an image: we wear a number of sets of lenses that influence our view of the events described in the biblical writings. Some of them color the facts, while others enlarge or distort them. But to be able to take them off we would first have to acknowledge that we have them on our noses in the first place. In what follows I want to describe some of these lenses that shrink our view of the genuine statements of the Pauline letters. Most of these lenses are already rather old, but they appear to be amazingly durable!

The Androcentric-Individualist Lens:
"Paul Is an Outstanding Individual and the Sole Author of the Letters"

Looking through this lens results in one of the most consequential false views, with fundamental significance for the interpretation of Paul. We speak of "Paul's letters" without realizing that the letters themselves contain other references. Sometimes they indicate a whole collective of authors (cf. Crüsemann 1998, 655), for example in 1 Corinthians: "Paul and Sosthenes to the church that is in Corinth," 2 Corinthians and Philippians: "Paul and Timothy . . ." or Galatians: "Paul and all the brothers who are with me, to all the churches in Galatia" (here we must suppose that he simply fails to mention the sisters: cf. NRSV, "all the members of God's family," interpreting *adelphoi* inclusively), or 1 Thessalonians: "Paul, Sylvanus, and Timothy . . . ." From these various greetings it is clear both that the letters were not written by a single person and that they are not addressed to individuals.

On close inspection we see that even the so-called private letter to Philemon is also addressed to a community group represented by several people: "Apphia our sister and Archippus, our fellow-soldier, and the church in your house." In the history of interpretation this

---

[1] Edgar Hennecke and Wilhelm Schneemelcher, eds., *New Testament Apocrypha.* English translation supervised by Robert McL. Wilson (2nd rev. ed. Louisville: Westminster/John Knox, 1992) 2:239–46.

group is often made invisible and thus insignificant: Apphia is supposed to be Philemon's wife, and the letter a private matter between Paul and Philemon in which they deal with the escaped slave Onesimus. But Philemon is not the only person Paul addresses; instead, he is part of the network of relationships constituted by the house church, which figures as a counter-public to the state, and which is affected as a whole by the question of receiving Onesimus back (cf. Bieberstein 1998, 677). The fact that Apphia is singled out to be addressed personally as a witness who will make sure that Philemon behaves as Paul expects him to "opens a 'window' on traditions about women in the early communities that have been rendered invisible" (ibid.).

Scholars have for a long time presumed, as far as the gospels are concerned, that they were not written by individuals, but by a substantial group of people who use them to tell their stories, their experiences and their hopes, and their conflicts as well. Luise Schottroff calls the gospels the "songbook of the poor" to emphasize their communitarian character and their origins (Schottroff 1995, 207). The context in which Paul's letters originated is the communities that desired to live a life in accordance with the Torah and in faith in Jesus the Messiah. Paul always worked with other women and men, and traveled with a number of them; he lived with others in their house churches. To name only the most familiar, there were Prisca and Aquila, Junia and Andronicus, Phoebe, Timothy and Silas, Chloe, Lydia, Thecla. In many of the communities with which he had contact he was confronted with the presence and active participation of a number of independent women. He certainly argued with them and taught them, but he had to listen to what they had to say as well. The respect he shows for the numerous women he mentions, for example, in the greetings list in Romans 16 gives us a glimpse of a network of relationships in which he was not simply the patriarchal top dog. On the contrary! The living vision of *koinonia* in the communities, a communion of equals based on mutuality, is also visible in the background of many expressions in Paul's letters. For Paul it was a reality with which, for example in the case of equal roles for women, he frequently struggled.

The Dogmatic Lens:
"Paul Alone Represents the True Gospel"

If we once take off the first (androcentric/individual) glasses, we will not keep the second on our noses much longer. If I start with the idea of a network of relationships in which theological, practical, and political questions are argued I quickly begin to doubt whether Paul really published his own dogmatic theology in these letters. Many of his statements were uttered in a particular context, often as a fairly vehement contribution to the discussion, but they should not be misunderstood as timelessly valid truths.

An approach that understands Paul's statements as contextual also calls into question a practice that is rather common among us, one that frequently confronts those who attend church regularly. The choice of preaching texts tends to create the feeling that I can pick out individual portions of the text and understand them. Sermons on texts from Paul, in particular, often serve to formulate a quintessence out of which the preacher as quickly as possible discovers a springboard to the universal truths that stand behind it. Caution is warranted! Many statements are made false when they are ripped out of context, but especially when they are confused with dogmatic utterances.

The Lens of Malestream Theology of the Victors: "Paul is the Founder of the Christian Church. He Speaks from a Position of Power and Universally Acknowledged Authority."

In principle, the question of undisputed authority has already been answered, but to this point it has been examined only from the intra-community perspective. We must now turn to a broader perspective: the situation of the Jewish communities that believed in Jesus Messiah before the destruction of the Temple in 70 C.E. When we speak of Christianity we are frequently influenced (without really being aware of it) by the fact that it became the state religion in the fourth century, and thus achieved its ultimate triumph. We see Christianity from the perspective of the victors, within a history in which the church has power and influence and feels itself superior to others.

In an essay on the Letter to the Galatians, Brigitte Kahl poses the question: "Can we imagine a Paul who was not thinking about opposition between Jews and Christians, but still about the contrast between Jews and Gentiles? . . . whose 'Christianity' represents a radical-messianic variant of Judaism before the destruction of the second Temple?" (Kahl 1998, 604). We know the sequence of historical events: the catastrophe of 70, the destruction of the Bar-Kochba revolt in 135, Marcion, Constantine. . . . But in Paul's lifetime the situation was entirely different. The Jesus movement and the communities in which Paul was at home were a part of the Jewish liberation struggle against the Roman empire; they were a Jewish liberation movement alongside others within the Pax Romana. Can we imagine a Paul who stands on the side of the "Jewish losers"? Brigitte Kahl calls for a rereading of Paul's letters: "The more critically we read our post-Roman, Western Christian winners' history from the perspective of the losers, the sooner we can penetrate this 'hermeneutical wall of silence' and learn to read Paul in a new way" (ibid.).

Think of Paul: a Jew who pled for an inclusive Judaism in which Jews and people of the nations have a place where they can live a new, messianic praxis of reconciliation and solidarity. They live this intercultural peace under the sign of the cross and not that of the emperor! (cf. Kahl 1998, 606). Paul's program for this kind of world was a failure. At the latest with the Constantinian triumph the church placed itself on the side of political power and abandoned its idea of a reconciliation of peoples. The consequence was a history of injustice in the name of the Cross, reaching its gruesome climax in the church's coresponsibility for the persecution and murder of millions of Jews in Auschwitz and other places during the era of National Socialism.

An interpretation of Paul that locates him within the framework of the Judaism of his own time must get behind this triumphalistic history. A Paul on the side of the Jewish losers, living out the hopes and visions of a tiny, oppressed, and persecuted minority—such a Paul is closer to me than the church leader of our tradition. His vision of a common life shared by different people of varied origins in light of the reign of God is something I can apply to our own situation, as a defense against every kind of fundamentalism and isolation from others.

Pauline Visions

When I work with the biblical texts today I must admit that I deliberately look at them through at least one lens: that of my feminist liberation theology, which makes me especially partisan on behalf of the needs of women. At this point I want to thank Luise Schottroff for the special polishing this lens has received through her work. Her enthusiasm for the Bible has caused me at times to look at it anew and to discover many important aspects. The dominant theology still asserts that this lens distorts the so-called objective view and makes the results unscholarly. But I think that it makes our view of the historical events clearer and renders us more sensitive to ways in which the biblical narratives and letters can become living texts for us also, witnesses that can move us with their language of hope and resistance.

On almost every page of his letters Paul tells us that we are justified, that we no longer need to allow ourselves to be held captive by sinful structures, that we can act—that we have the freedom to do this, and God's support as well. From his letters I learn that faith in God and the praxis of justice go together inseparably. They challenge us to become irritating, out-of-line Pauls and Paulas, impatient sisters of Lydia, who shout into the muffling silence: "For freedom Christ has set us free.

Stand firm, therefore, and do not submit again to a yoke of slavery" (Gal 5:1). We can make good use of the Pauline texts to insure that our voices become louder and are heard once more, even outside the narrow walls of our churches and theology departments; they can be to us a source of courage and of consolation.

Bibliography

Bieberstein, Sabine. "Der Brief an Philemon. Brieflektüre unter den kritischen Augen Apphias," in Luise Schottroff and Marie-Theres Wacker, eds., *Kompendium Feministische Bibelauslegung*. Gütersloh: Chr.Kaiser/Gütersloher Verlagshaus, 1998, 676–82.

Crüsemann, Marlene. "Der zweite Brief an die Gemeinde in Thessalonich. Hoffen auf das gerechte Gericht Gottes," in ibid., 654–60.

Jensen, Anne. *Thekla – die Apostolin. Ein apokrypher Text neu entdeckt, übersetzt und kommentiert von Anne Jensen.* Freiburg: Herder, 1995.

Kahl, Brigitte. "Der Brief an die Gemeinde in Galatien. Vom Unbehagen der Geschlechter und anderen Problemen des Andersseins," in Schottroff and Wacker, eds., *Kompendium Feministische Bibelauslegung*, 603–11.

Käsemann, Ernst. "Begründet der neutestamentliche Kanon die Einheit der Kirche?" (1951), in idem, *Exegetische Versuche und Besinnungen: Auswahl.* Göttingen: Vandenhoeck & Ruprecht, 1986, 86–95.

Schottroff, Luise. "Auf dem Weg zu einer feministischen Rekonstruktion der Geschichte des frühen Christentums," in Luise Schottroff, Silvia Schroer, and Marie-Theres Wacker, *Feministische Exegese. Forschungserträge zur Bibel aus der Perspektive von Frauen.* Darmstadt: Wissenschaftliche Buchgesellschaft, 1995, 175–248. English: "Toward a Feminist Reconstruction of the History of Early Christianity," in Luise Schottroff, Silvia Schroer, and Marie-Theres Wacker, *Feminist Interpretation. The Bible in Women's Perspective.* Translated by Martin and Barbara Rumscheidt. Minneapolis: Fortress, 1998, 179–254.

Marlene Crüsemann

Living Water:
Elements of a Feminist Proclamation
According to John 4

> *"Everything stems from enthusiasm and love.*
> *And that this is true of our life*
> *is something very beautiful—*
> *perhaps the most beautiful thing of all."*
>
> —Theodor Fontane

"For with you is the fountain of life"—these words addressed to God in Ps 36:9 have become one of the most celebrated images for the womanliness of God in feminist theology and liturgy. The idea of gushing life coming to us, inexhaustibly, from God and enabling our life through the watering of barren land, dried-up gardens, the thirsty throat offers many women a new and reliable way of access to God. In the following pages, when I ask about the elements of a feminist proclamation, it seems to me that one New Testament portrait of a woman is especially well suited to bind together this image of God and women's activity of teaching and preaching. I am referring to the story of the calling of the Samaritan woman in John 4:1-42, who proclaims Jesus Messiah to her people. The turning point in her existence comes with the gift of living water, which becomes a fountain within her welling up to eternal life. The mysterious concepts of the Fourth Gospel can lead us some distance along the way to a feminist homiletics, which is just beginning to emerge (cf. Köhler 1996). The text offers me three important truths about the condition, the content, and the effects of women's preaching that can be called feminist.

The Condition:
Liberation and Living Water

At the beginning is liberation. The first one in this story who crosses the line is Jesus, who passes through the heartland of Samaria and by Mount Gerizim on his way to Galilee. During a midday rest at Jacob's well, between Sychar and ancient Sichem, he acquires a Samaritan woman disciple by first asking her for water to quench his thirst. It has scarcely been recognized heretofore that this is a "call" scene, but the Fourth Gospel makes that abundantly clear: the detailed description of Jesus' encounter with the Samaritan woman is built up using the same motifs and key words as the calling of the disciples in ch. 1. Jesus shows himself to be a personal prophet who quickly and existentially knows his own (1:47-48; 4:17-19). As a result, the disciples in both cases explicitly acknowledge Jesus as the Messiah (with the title itself translated, 1:41; 4:25-26). Finally, the newfound Messiah is pointed out to others with the words: "Come and see," with the addition of variable concepts designed to draw the different audiences into this knowledge (1:46; 4:29; cf. 1:39). In the speech with which the Samaritan woman herself appears in public (4:29) all these elements are brought together. She thus appears as the called and exemplary disciple of her people, and their missionary.

We are indebted to Luise Schottroff's social-historical investigation of this story for the fact that this woman of Sychar no longer needs to slink through exegesis as a loose-living "slut," but has been given back her dignity as a fivefold widow or divorced woman and a hard-working drawer of water (Schottroff 1992). Because of the impossibility for a woman to survive alone in ancient patriarchal society, every familial catastrophe had to be followed as quickly as possible by a new marriage. Because the woman was without the security that her current life-partner was not ready to afford her in full degree, and she is able to say, "I have no husband" (v. 17), we become aware of the immediate efficacy of the "water" that Jesus promises, and that she, understanding, asks of him (v. 15). She names her personal life-situation, which enslaves her, leaves its symbol, the water jar, behind her for good (v. 28), and takes her leave in the freedom of her new, messianic existence as a witness.

What would we call freedom in the situations of those women called to witness today? Working as "water drawers" in today's church means representing the unaltered patriarchal church, with its continuing male hierarchy, to the world as apparently humane, kind, and feminine, in order that the membership numbers may be more or less sustained. But beautiful liturgies and warm-hearted sermons by women, taking place within a largely woman-alienated and womanless church decision-making and leadership structure, can help to secure it in place. Is this due to the timidity and unfreedom of a feminist preaching that is content with what has been achieved and does not desire to rub anyone the wrong way? When the critical element, the word that separates, is absent we will go on dragging ourselves through an institutional church built and resting on a base of useful water-drawers.

But if we "leave our water jars" and assert: "I have no husband," it means that we are willing and able to do without male protection in scholarship and church teaching. This action should be carried out deliberately and repeatedly. We are and remain essentially "women out of line," as Ulrike Wagner-Rau says, adopting a phrase of Hedwig Meyer-Wilmes': women theologians and pastors are in "a tense situation, for the rifts and tensions that, at present, shape the relationship of many women to the Christian church, traverse their own persons: They are representatives of the thing they are criticizing. Their identification with the tradition is fractured. They are out of line in more ways than one, and therefore they are never really at home" (Wagner-Rau 1992, 16). This life on the line can be chosen deliberately and freely, in reliance on the water of life that is given to us, a fountain that never dries up. Live women theologians will then no longer be going around as "everybody's darling." They will find the critical word at the right moment, independent, ready to risk, shucking off accommodation and dependency.

In this connection Jesus' gift of "living water," which becomes a source within the recipient, in this case the Samaritan woman (v. 14), is of interest. We are inclined to think of the gift of autonomy, independence, inexhaustible strength and enduring creativity, such as she experiences as she begins her preaching activity. It becomes concrete in the vivacity and down-to-earth quality of women's preaching: It can liquefy and release what has been stopped up, making knots and hardenings soft and pliant for living processes because it is interested in living processes, especially in women's material everyday life and that of their families. This is the sense in which I understand the epigraph given above, about enthusiasm and love that permits life to flow out into true vivacity and inspiration.

Even if we can scarcely grasp the full content of the Johannine combination of "water" and "eternal life," Tillich's formula, "unambiguous life," synonymous with eternal life, may help us a little farther. It means a recourse to our true existence, away from the alienation brought about by all kinds of diminishment of life and distance from God (Tillich 1963). In the theory and praxis of a feminist liberation theology, for example, women's groups acquire great importance when they enable individual women to achieve healing and liberation from their often alienating existence in unjust and unbearable family structures. It is no accident that, for women, word images with motifs of water and fountains play a major role in the names given to places of restoration and healing.

The first indication of the Samaritan woman's "living water," which she receives and can give to others, can be derived indirectly from the scene at the well: in the course of the story, and at the end, nothing more is said of Jesus' thirst. Such a dialogue drives away ordinary thirst as well as thirst for genuine life in a mutuality of giving and receiving. But let us allow Jesus himself to instruct us more fully about the true context from which "living water" flows to us.

The Content: A Jewish Messiah

At the center of feminist preaching, as to its content, and because of John 4, stands the Jewish Messiah, Jesus, who only as such can be Savior and "Redeemer" of the world (v. 42). It is a question of the interpretation of the fundamental statement: "salvation comes from the Jews" (v. 22), with which Jesus indicates to the Samaritan woman the true locus of all knowledge of God. She recognizes this and, according to the Fourth Gospel, thus becomes the person in whom the overcoming of the centuries-long division between the Samaritan and Jewish people begins.

It is certainly possible to view the alienation of the later Gentile Christian church from Judaism as a distant analogy to the Samaritan-Jewish story. We can see in the Samaritan woman a prototype for a way to acknowledge the unconditional priority of Israel's experience of God over our own. But in the intervening years, through the error of Antijudaism, we have distanced ourselves much farther from Judaism than the Samaritans, who in fact, on the basis of their heritage and religious practice, regarded themselves as Israel. Their sacred scriptures were simply the Torah, which thereby, especially as "the Law," acquired a very different and contrary status to what it assumed in Christianity. The "Shema Israel" (Deut 6:4-9), the call to confess that God is one, and the Song at the Sea in Exodus 15, sung by the prophet Miriam at the departure of the children of Israel from Egypt, were from ancient times principal texts for Samaritan faith. This is evident from synagogal inscriptions in many places throughout the Mediterranean, and especially in the land of Israel in the Hellenistic-Roman period (Kippenberg 1971, 150ff.). We Christians from among the Gentiles, in contrast, were only introduced into Israel's Exodus story through Jesus. We can participate in it on the basis of our own new experiences, when we take to heart Jesus' teaching about the origins of our salvation, which comes from the Jews.

Thus we can only discover what exodus and liberation mean through Jesus' word to us and our acknowledgment of Israel's enduring priority. Connected to this is the necessity of learning from the Torah. The Fourth Gospel also associates belief in Jesus' messianic character with the interpretation and understanding of Scripture and the prophets. Especially when we attempt to interpret his words about "living water" out attention is drawn to Scripture: ". . . let the one who believes in me drink. *As the scripture has said*, 'Out of the believer's heart shall flow rivers of living water'" (John 7:38). Jesus, as a pious Jew, attends the Feast of Booths in Jerusalem and there, in the Temple, shows himself a master of scriptural interpretation (7:14-24). He demonstrates that it is not a question of himself and his own teaching, but of God, the discovery of God's will, and keeping the Torah (v. 19). This pattern of preaching, devoid of any kind of self-aggrandizement, is repeated by those whom Jesus calls, especially the Samaritan woman.

The saying about the water is a citation of Deutero-Isaiah, recalling his teaching regarding the second Exodus of the people of Israel out of their Babylonian captivity: "Let anyone who is thirsty come to me, and let the one who believes in me drink." "Ho, everyone who thirsts, come to the waters" (John 7:37/Isa 55:1). This associative reading of Scripture makes it clear where we can always seek the "living water," here in our own liberation and in the doing of justice, for there is also an echo of Deutero-Isaiah's sermon on fasting, with its challenge to feed and clothe those in need and to care for those who suffer: *"you shall be like a watered garden, like a spring of water, whose waters never fail"* (Isa 58:11). In addition, we are in touch with our erotic power and ability to love: *"a garden fountain, a well of living water, and flowing streams from Lebanon"* (Song 4:15).

Such associations show that absurd examples of Antijudaism that assert, among other things, that for "John" Jesus, as God's personified Wisdom, takes the place of the Law (Brown 1966, 179) are unnecessary and can very easily be deprived of any force through an examination of the text itself. A departure from Antijudaism can be easier for us, as feminist theologians, than for traditional exegesis, because we are already used to abandoning previously normative paradigms and systems, including the patriarchal. We are on the way to an interpretation of the Bible and, still more difficult, the New Testament, without deep-seated anti-Jewish stereotypes, and in an effort to perceive the more subtle forms before it is too late. But behold, it appears to be possible, and to bring with it as well a surprising gain in content (cf. especially Henze, Janssen, Müller, and Wehn 1997).

Feminist preaching must ultimately measure the whole of Christian proclamation by whether it contributes to the consolation of Israel. For according to the prophet Jeremiah the renewed covenant serves for the awakening and consoling of the dishonored and sorrowing people Israel, which is the first to receive the lifegiving water: *"They shall come and sing aloud on the height of Zion, and they shall be radiant over the goodness of the LORD, over the grain, the wine, and the oil, and over the young of the flock and the herd; their life shall become like a watered garden, and they shall never languish again"* (Jer 31:12).

The Effects: Coming and Seeing for Oneself

By her preaching the Samaritan woman sows the Messiah in the land of Samaria, where the other disciples are later to reap (v. 38; cf. Dollar 1983, 106–107). But the effects of her preaching are doubly astounding: "Many Samaritans from that city believed in him because of the woman's testimony" (v. 39), but then no longer because of her, "for we have heard for ourselves, and we know" (v. 42). It seems that she is pushed away, set aside by those who had previously listened to her. It would be worth investigating what the historical facts behind this were, but in the present context that is of secondary importance. I think it is this very thing that furnishes a model and direction for effective preaching by women: They enable the hearers themselves to see and judge; they do not get in the way of their independence; they do not prevent them from getting along without themselves, the initiators. This is in harmony with an understanding of "selflessness" that Christine Schaumberger has derived through her critical-constructive revision of this and other virtues previously considered "feminine" (Schaumberger 1988, 277ff.): "'Selflessness could be a *productive strength* for a woman who herself sets in motion life, activities, work with her whole strength, but also allows them to develop further on their own, without her control, sometimes even against her goals and without being 'grateful'" (ibid. 278).

The continually recurring expression of a male-dominated history of office reveals almost the opposite. Since the earliest reception of Paul's letters, word and gospel have been too closely tied to the person of the witness, and at the latest since Luther's day they have been quite literally identified with a person and her or his experiences. But a truly evangelical preaching says in essence: "Come and see for yourself." It took an important initial step in the work of the Samaritan woman. This corresponds to a feminist concept of leadership, including church leadership, as Luise Schottroff has expounded it in view of Lydia's example, and brought to reality in her own work: Lydia's "leadership arose when she brought people together into a community that was first oriented on the God of Israel and then on Jesus. . . . The power growing in this community was not the kind that makes others small but a power that is shared and wants to make others great when they are small and in misery" (Schottroff 1993, 136).

Thus it is not necessary to elevate oneself and to make one's own work the medium for others' knowledge of God. We should reject the practice, found even in some feminist circles, of constantly stressing one's own service since we believe it to be a male custom worth our imitation because some men do it successfully, or because it is part of a strong feminine consciousness. On the contrary, selfless encouragement and empowerment serves an independent knowledge on the part of all those addressed. It contrasts with the ambition of many "men of God," and even some "women of God." The unique message of the Samaritan woman for a homiletic theory consists in "her" gospel, which is remembered without our knowing her name, in the form of an independence that she evokes in others.

In light of the fundamental, experiential stance of feminist theory and theology, it follows that one's own experience, the source of the knowledge of individual women and groups, cannot and should not be generalized. My experience is a woman's experience, but not the experience of all women and hence not to be universalized without limit. This was clearly shown by the protest of women from Latin America, Asia, and Africa against white European and American women's thoughtlessly declaring their specific experiences of oppression to be paradigmatic for all. In particular, the voices of Black womanist theologians have pointed this out to us (cf. Schaumberger 1988, 222ff.).

The story of the Samaritan woman illustrates the difference, and the need for differentiation, in life-experiences, the variety in the life circumstances of women. When the inhabitants of Sychar refuse to listen only to the "aha" experience of their water-bearing fellow citizen as proof of the reliability of the message of the Messiah they are insisting on the value and power of proof in their own, immediate, and probably very different experiences. In principle the first Samaritan woman knows this, too: "Come and see!" The living water of her testimony brings the others to their own, immediate experience of the true Life.

Bibliography

Brown, Raymond E. *The Gospel According to John I (I–XII)*. AB 29. Garden City, N.Y.: Doubleday, 1966.

Dexinger, Ferdinand, and Reinhard Pummer, eds. *Die Samaritaner*. WdF 604. Darmstadt: Wissenschaftliche Buchgesellschaft, 1991.

Dollar, Stephen E. *The Significance of Women in the Fourth Gospel*. Unpublished dissertation. New Orleans Baptist Seminary, 1983.

Henze, Dagmar, Claudia Janssen, Stefanie Müller, and Beate Wehn. *Antijudaismus im Neuen Testament? Grundlagen für die Arbeit mit biblischen Texten*. Gütersloh: Chr. Kaiser, 1997.

Kippenberg, Hans Gerhard. *Garizim und Synagoge. Traditionsgeschichtliche Untersuchungen zur samaritanischen Religion der aramäischen Periode*. Berlin and New York: Walter de Gruyter, 1971.

Köhler, Wiebke. "Homiletik – feministisch?! Predigerin und Hörerin als überfälliges Thema der Homiletik," *Wege zum Menschen* 48 (1996) 132–50.

Schaumberger, Christine. "Subversive Bekehrung, Schulderkenntnis, Schwesterlichkeit, Frauenmacht: Irritierende und inspirierende Grundmotive kritisch-feministischer Befreiungstheologie," in Christine Schaumberger and Luise Schottroff, *Schuld und Macht. Studien zu einer feministischen Befreiungstheologie*. Munich: Kaiser, 1988, 153–288.

Schottroff, Luise. "Die Samaritanerin am Brunnen (Joh 4)," in Renate Jost, Rainer Kessler, and Christoph M. Raisig, eds., *Auf Israel hören. Sozialgeschichtliche Bibelauslegungen*. Luzern: 1992, 105–32.

————. "Lydia. Eine neue Qualität der Macht," in Luise Schottroff, *Befreiungserfahrungen. Studien zur Sozialgeschichte des Neuen Testaments*. ThB 82. Munich: Kaiser, 1990, 305–09. English: "Lydia: A New Quality of Power," in Luise Schottroff, *Let the Oppressed Go Free. Feminist Perspectives on the New Testament*. Translated by Annemarie S. Kidder. Louisville: Westminster John Knox, 1993.

Tillich, Paul. *Systematic Theology 3: Life and the Spirit. History and the Kingdom of God*. Chicago: University of Chicago Press, 1963.

Wagner-Rau, Ulrike. *Zwischen Vaterwelt und Feminismus. Eine Studie zur pastoralen Identität von Frauen*. Gütersloh: Gerd Mohn, 1992.

Dagmar Henze

Peter: A Transgressor in His Own Time

In the following sermon I want to address Acts 10:1-34, a text that is commonly interpreted in anti-Jewish fashion. In Acts 10 interpreters see "a paradigmatic Gentile conversion" and, following the supposed plan of Acts, speak of the "transfer of salvation from the Jews to the Gentiles." The traditional interpretation concentrates on the person of Cornelius and the divine miracle of his baptism. In this kind of interpretation Peter remains in the background. His experiences are, for the most part, given short shrift. Peter's visions are interpreted as Christianity's fundamental rejection of Jewish food laws. In my sermon I have attempted to fix a different focus. Not Cornelius, but Peter is the principal figure in the narrative. In spite of his resistance to any change in his faith he is here led to think again about the cultic barriers between people of Jewish and non-Jewish origins. Acts 10 should thus be set within the halakic discussion about the significance and obligatory nature of the food laws in early Jewish-Christian communities. Kashruth, the food laws of Judaism, are among the most complicated of the rituals and ordinances in which Judaism is so rich. They regulate the selection, preparation, and consumption of food and are traced to commands in the Torah.

Behind kashruth stands the belief that external signs have symbolic value and confessional character; consequently, religion is never something purely interior. Signs create an atmosphere in which religion saturates daily living and the whole of life. In the religious life the kitchen is not something incidental; it is a central location. A strict observance of the purity code was important for Israel especially during times of foreign occupation and oppression. Purity, that is, the holiness of the nation, was the precondition for God's presence and thus also for God's help for the people, on which it was particularly dependent in times of oppression. Keeping the purity code ensured the identity of the Jewish people from within.

Throughout my sermon one finds the theme of borders, lines drawn by faith. In this I hope I have found a key to making the significance of the purity code in the earliest communities, so difficult for us to imagine, somehow understandable for people of our own time. I preached the sermon in January 1996 in the congregation in Hannover Münden where I was serving my vicariate. At that time I was already working as a graduate assistant to Luise Schottroff at the University of Kassel. There I learned the theology on which the following sermon is based.

Dear Friends,

I still remember it very well: I was a child, standing on the border. You all know it, right over there, near Witzenhausen, across the Werra: you could see it—the border to what was then the D.D.R. You saw the fence, with the barbed wire on top, and the striped no-man's-land behind it. I often stood there with my parents and looked across. Borders divide not only countries, but more particularly people: my grandmother from her sister, my father from his cousin. Borders separate parents from their children, those who once were friends and those who never could be friends because the border stood between them.

It's years now since the wall came down. But there is still a border between East and West, especially in my generation—walls that often make it impossible for people to approach each other because they seem to see something threatening or strange in the other person. Borders like that exist not only between East and West. I often sense them when I encounter people who make me nervous because they look different—for example, the homeless who sit down there in front of St. Blaise's Church in the summer. It is hard to overcome such barriers within one's own heart. People have known that for millennia; we even find it in the Bible.

Let me tell you a story about how Peter had to cross a border, a barrier within his own heart, even within his own faith.

Dear Friends, our story begins when Peter, one day when he was visiting Simon the tanner, was sitting on the roof. It was about noon. The sun was high in the sky. There was a biting smell of freshly-tanned leather in the air. It was terribly hot. Peter was dozing. He felt weak, his stomach was growling; he was hungry. Suddenly it seemed to him that something was coming down out of the sky—a big, white cloth. In the cloth were all sorts of animals, clean and unclean: that is, those that Peter, who like many Christians in the first communities was a pious Jew and lived according to the food laws of the Torah, could eat, but also those that one was not supposed to eat. Peter heard a voice saying: "Kill and eat!" He was shocked. "It is the tempter, the devil. God wants to test me, as Jesus was tempted in the desert. No, no, I will stand firm."

Peter looked at the sun. There it was again: the same cloth, again with all the animals, the clean and the unclean, in it. And then he heard a voice saying: "What God has made clean, you must not call profane!" The cloth then appeared again in the sky. Odd, the same dream three times.

While Peter was still thinking about his dream he heard three men below at the door of the house, asking for him. And again he heard a voice from heaven: "Look, three men are searching for you. Now get up, go down, and go with them without hesitation, for I have sent them." Still in a fog, he went down the stairs: "Go down! Eat! Don't hesitate! God has made it clean!" Everything was going around and around in his head.

At the door stood three men, a Roman soldier and two of his servants. Peter said faintly: "I am the one you are looking for; what is the reason for your coming?" The soldier answered: "Cornelius, a centurion, an upright and God-fearing man, our master, was directed by a holy angel to send for you to come to his house." Now Peter was really confused. A Roman centurion had sent for him. And an angel was mixed up in it somehow. Something was going on here. Peter looked around. The sun was sinking in a red sky at the horizon. It was already late. He asked the men to come into the house.

That night he couldn't sleep. Should he really go with these men to Caesarea? Should he really go to Cornelius, the Roman centurion? His mind went around and around. "No, I can't do that. After all, Cornelius is one of our enemies, one of those who have occupied our country. How much misery the Romans have already brought on this land! And then, Cornelius—well, the soldiers did say that he believes in our God, but probably in his own way. He certainly doesn't keep the commandments; he is unclean. I don't want to associate with anyone like that. People who do not keep the Torah are taboo for me. My God and my faith are important to me. I can't cross the boundaries of my faith. That can't be God's will."

Peter was miserable. He tossed and turned. He heard noises. The rattling of pots: Simon and his wife must be up already. It was nearly morning. Should he go, must he go? But if he was really honest with himself, he was terribly afraid to go. What would happen to him? How would he, a simple fisherman, be able to talk to a Roman centurion? Probably he wouldn't be able to utter a word. He would make a fool of himself for sure.

But little by little it became clear to him that the dream, the voice could not have been an accident. He couldn't exactly explain it, but somehow he had the feeling that he had to cross the boundary between himself and this foreigner who did not believe in Jesus. The next day he got up and went with Cornelius's soldiers, all the way to Caesarea. Some of his fellow believers went with him, which made Peter especially happy. When they got to Caesarea, after two days on the road, tired and worn out, Cornelius was waiting for them. The moment of encounter: Peter, a simple fisherman, and Cornelius, a Roman centurion; Peter, deeply rooted in his faith, and Cornelius, a seeker, someone who did not exactly know what he ought to believe, stood face to face. It was Cornelius who took the first step toward Peter. He threw himself in the dust at Peter's feet. He wanted to honor him as he had learned to do in Rome. But Peter said: "No, stand up. I am only a human being like you." He lifted him up and they looked into each other's eyes.

Together they entered the house. First Peter spoke; then he listened to Cornelius's story. Cornelius told him in detail how the angel had appeared and spoken to him, telling him to have Peter brought to him. Cornelius got very involved in his story. Joyful anticipation was written on his face: "Now, Peter, tell us what you have to say." Peter was uncertain. He looked around the room. A large number of people sat there, relatives and friends of Cornelius. None of them was a member of the Jewish people.

Images from his dream, images of the cloth and the animals, clean and unclean mixed together, surfaced suddenly before his eyes. Slowly, Peter became aware of the full enormity of the situation. He began to understand what God wanted to show him: the vision was not about animals, but about people! He stammered a little as he brought it out: "That's it! God wants me not to despise any person or call them unclean. That must be why I am here, and why I did not refuse when you came to get me. And here, with you, it has become clear to me: God does not regard persons, has no partiality, but takes pleasure in everyone from every nation who fears God and does justice."

For Peter this was unbelievable: here in the house of Cornelius, the stranger, the foreigner, the non-Christian, he was learning something new about his own God: God does not draw lines that exclude people. Peter had to struggle with himself. At first it appeared that doubt, questions, and fear would win the day. It was not so easy to find the courage to go to a Roman, a foreigner. And it was not a simple matter to change what was closest to his heart, his faith.

I find it consoling to see that God did not leave Peter alone at the frontiers of his faith, but led him and accompanied him. And God took a lot of trouble over Peter. Three times God sent him dreams, telling him again and again: "Don't hesitate!" Peter didn't cooperate until the soldiers came for him, and even then the angel of God played a part in the affair.

Only in that way did it come about that Peter went to Cornelius. Led by God, he was able to take the difficult and fearful road to another human being, a stranger. I am fascinated by this meeting. Two people come together, or rather they are led to one another, the two of them different from the ground up; normally they would probably have nothing to say to each other, but in our story they converse, and above all, they listen to each other. They don't want to change each other. Peter has not come as a missionary to Cornelius.

But what Peter would never have thought possible has taken place: in this very encounter across barriers with another who is not a Christian, *Peter* has learned something new about God: God does not regard persons, no matter what nation they come from; anyone who fears God and does right is pleasing to God.

Irene Dannemann

The Slave Woman's Challenge to Peter

The title of this essay refers to a biblical story from the New Testament. But you will not find it under this title in any Bible translation. The concordance does not include any biblical passages under the words "slave woman." Peter is easier to find, and a reader who is so inclined could discover, by working her way through the stories about Peter, which woman is referred to: the one called a "maid" in Luther's translation, "servant-girl" in the NRSV. Because the title I have chosen for the essay refers to a single woman, the search points to a story in Mark's gospel, at 14:66-72. That gets us over the first hurdle, and the effort required shows paradigmatically how difficult it becomes when a feminist perspective alters our view of the texts and new foci crystallize within them. We find ourselves outside the dominant rules for thinking and we have to explain what we mean. It is not always easy to maintain the position of outsider over the long haul. But it is certainly fun to experience how, again and again, others come to "aha" realizations.

I deliberately chose this inconvenient title for my contribution to this Festschrift for Luise Schottroff. I want to develop my ideas creatively, as we did in the doctoral seminar, in the feminist-liberation theology center at Kassel, or when we sat together at conferences and in vehement discussions dis-covered and developed possibilities for interpretation.

So that the reader can more easily follow my thought, I will begin with my own translation of Mark 14:66-72:

> While Peter was below in the courtyard one of the high priest's
> slave women came by. When she saw Peter warming himself she
> stared at him and said: "You also were with the man from Nazareth,
> Jesus." But he denied it, saying: "I do not know or understand
> what you are talking about." And he went out into the forecourt,

and a cock crowed. And when the slave woman saw him she again began to say to the bystanders: "This man is one of them!" But he went on denying it. And soon afterward the bystanders again said to Peter: "Certainly you are one of them, for you are a Galilean, too." But he began to curse and to swear: "I do not know this man you are talking about!" And immediately the cock crowed for the second time. And Peter remembered that Jesus had said to him, "Before the cock crows twice, you will deny me three times." And he broke down and wept for a long time.

It is not clear in the narrative just why the slave woman speaks to Peter. Does she notice this foreigner while she is working in the courtyard? Is her attention drawn to him because he is neither a soldier nor one of the servants? Does she see that he is standing apart? Or is she just asking out of curiosity?

After Jesus' arrest the courtyard of the high priest's palace had come wide awake: a lot of people are standing around talking. At last, that troublemaker has been captured—a success worth celebrating. Slaves, both women and men, and other people employed in the high priest's household are busy: stirring up the fire in case there is a need to offer food and drink. The servants are rushing back and forth. So it is easy to understand why the slave woman speaks twice to Peter. We cannot know whether she saw him just twice or whether she noticed him again and again as she hurried to and fro. Whatever the case, she addresses him a second time in the outer courtyard, and we hear nothing about her intention: is she annoyed that he is still hanging around the palace, even though he had denied what she suspected? Is her curiosity aroused by this man's lie? After all, unlike her he is free, and male besides.

We can only fill the text's silence with our suppositions. The protagonist's purposes remain opaque to us. But the text does tell us something that is generally overlooked and yet constitutes the point of the narrative: Here in the palace the slave woman is known, and her word is worth more than Peter's. Nevertheless, she does not directly accuse him or denounce him. She does not turn to any of the armed men standing about and demand: "Seize him, he is one of them. You can kill two birds with one stone." She speaks to Peter, but she does not betray him to the soldiers. She could, but she does not. She lets Peter get away. Because the slave woman does not insist on his arrest, Peter saves his life.

We did a bibliodrama of this scene in a university seminar. The students expected that in the scene in the high priest's palace courtyard Peter would draw all the attention. If it had been done in a theatre they would have aimed a spotlight at him as soon as he appeared. They would have placed him center stage and arranged the other characters around the foremost disciple and church founder. The traditional interpretation and title of the text passage as "Peter's Denial" was in their very blood. For them it was obvious that Peter was central—an interpretation that is set before us in imagery in all the illustrations of Peter with the rooster. The students also expected that all the activities in the courtyard would cease as soon as the slave woman spoke to Peter. They reacted with angry resistance when Peter only played an incidental role in the high priest's palace that night. Only after a vigorous discussion could the disciple be displaced from center stage to a corner. In the course of the class's work with the text the slave woman's double encounter with him was revealed as an incidental part of this night scene. Peter only attracts attention in the palace courtyard when the woman (and later the group of bystanders) takes notice of him. Thus the students' image of Peter changed: the image of the focal apostle was deconstructed.

This deconstruction involved not only the historical insight that neither Peter nor the community of disciples around Jesus nor the beginnings of early Christianity occupied the center of the Roman empire's attention. New aspects of the personality of this disciple were also discussed: for example, his bitter weeping also aroused the students' interest. It expresses his insight: "I have acted wrongly." He had to admit his own wrongdoing. After that, there can be a new beginning.

The image the biblical story sketches of the courtyard in the nighttime sets up a contrast with Jesus' trial before the Sanhedrin in the upper story of the palace. In terms of the narrative, both confrontations take place simultaneously: the slave woman argues with Peter down below in the courtyard, the high priest upstairs in the same house with Jesus. Jesus holds firmly to his message and does not distance himself from it. The high priest is able to bring the trial to a successful conclusion. In contrast, something entirely different happens below, in the courtyard: the slave woman challenges Peter to confess his discipleship. She does not do it in an official trial, but in the crowded courtyard, whose very fullness perhaps affords more anonymity than would be the case in a clearly visible dialogue. Unlike her owner, she does not insist on an arrest. She wants to know whether Peter belongs to Jesus' followers and has the courage to acknowledge it. But she does not stab him in the back when he denies everything. Thus she not only acts differently from her owner, but behaves in a disloyal manner with respect to her owner's interests, for he would certainly have been interested in seeing Jesus' talk about an inclusive vision of the reign of God be utterly silenced, and would want those ideas to be forgotten as quickly as possible.

In the story about the slave woman's demand that Peter confess who he is we are probably in touch with experiences that Mark's community had undergone. They knew how courts demanded of Christians who had been denounced to them: "Retract your confession of faith, or you will die." The community learned that confession of faith was a demand of daily life, not only in exceptional situations. In their everyday lives in the Roman empire the members of the Christian community learned to address one another as brother and sister, not to bow before the pagan temples, to abstain from meat offered to idols, and to stay away from the games and specifically non-Christian religious festivals. When, in the biblical story, an ordinary slave woman appears and challenges Peter, even brings him to deny his confession of faith, the community is meditating on the experience of daily exposure to danger. And people did not always have the courage and strength to stand fast to their confession.

The surprising conclusion to the story shows, moreover, that the demand for a confession need not always lead to arrest. Perhaps we see reflected here the experience that the community was protected, if at all, by slave women, and that it must find a way to speak its convictions, even when it was very dangerous to do so. Without talking about them it could not address and persuade other people.

In the congregation in Frankfurt where I am a pastor we recently had a group of Ghanaian visitors. They asked why there were so few young people and so many old people at the worship service—just the reverse of what they were used to at home. I answered that in my experience the Christian message seems very unmodern and "out" to young people. They have to steel themselves to admit that there is anything interesting for them in God or the Christian message. They are happy when, in Boy Scouts or Girl Scouts for example, they find that "there are lots of us; we're not even a minority. Here there are other people who have the same questions we have." In many of the schools the climate has changed so much that there is no interest at all in religion classes; they are not seen as enrichment, but as the first subject to be dropped because it is so unimportant. There is no parallel offering of courses in ethics as a substitute. As a pastor I am generally regarded by the high school students and teachers as an outsider—and I *am*. I share this experience with actively engaged colleagues who are sent by their churches to give religious instruction in the schools. Many teachers describe their primary instructional goal as giving information. They have given up on inculcating social or ethical competence in the children. From the children's responses I learn that I introduce themes at a personal and political level that are never broached in school otherwise. As time goes on, the children ask more and more of me. For them

I come into the school as a pastor, not an ordinary teacher, and they want to hear from me what the Christian message has to offer them—whether it has more to say to them than other religious messages. So I become bolder in what I say. Against the normality of everyday violence I plead for nonviolence and show its advantages. Against a resigned view of the personal and social future I struggle, together with the children, to discover powerful visions and actions. The children demand of me a confession of faith, which I must reaffirm for myself. For a long time I did not understand their questions as challenges to a faith confession, but dismissed them as odd. The persistence of the children who pursue me, as the slave woman did not allow Peter to escape responsibility, has changed me.

Not only the recitation of the creed during worship, but everyday speaking and acting are confessional (cf. Rom 12:1-3). This is about the way of discipleship, about acting justly, listening to others and paying attention to them and living together in peace. Whoever lives this way will continually rub people the wrong way and get crossways with both society and church. Every moment of our lives becomes important. It is never clear from the outset which moments will require of us a confessional stance, and which will not. "It is about every minute of our lives" (Adrienne Rich 1991, 50). The initiative for justice becomes a way of life that is never at rest.

Daily confessions are of many kinds: using inclusive language even when it is difficult; introducing examples involving girls even though they are not in the school or worship materials provided; clinging to hope for peace, justice, and equality, even though the signs of the times are against it; talking of Jesus' inclusive message of the reign of God, even though capitalistic market mechanisms are triumphant in every sphere of our lives and throughout the world. These are the confessions to which the story of the encounter between Peter and the slave woman two thousand years ago challenges me—with a surprising immediacy, if I allow myself to hear the question.

Bibliography

Dannemann, Irene. *Aus dem Rahmen fallen. Frauen im Markusevangelium. Eine feministische Re-Vision.* Berlin: Alektor, 1996.

Rich, Adrienne. "Der Kampf, mir meine Wahrnehmungen zu erhalten . . . Adrienne Rich im Gespräch mit Audre Lorde," in Dagmar Schutz, ed., *Macht und Sinnlichkeit. Ausgewählte Texte von Audre Lorde und Adrienne Rich.* 3rd expanded ed. Frankfurt: Orlanda Frauenverlag, 1983, 27–59.

Sigrid Lampe-Densky

Domitia, Marcia, and the Nameless Smuggler: Pearl Dealers in the Roman Empire

The Via Sacra, the holy street, was the main business thoroughfare in ancient Rome. Even today one can form an impression of it on a visit to the Roman Forum. Countless shops lined the street in those days, but there is scarcely a trace of them left. Aelius Aristides (2nd c. C.E.) proudly reports in his "Roman Address" that in the famed capital city of the Roman empire one could buy any kind of goods imaginable: "Brought there out of every land and sea was whatever the season produced, and the products of every land, river, and sea, as well as the arts of the Greeks and barbarians. Anyone who wants to see all that must either visit every corner of the earth in order to behold it, or come to this city [Rome]. For what grows and is produced among the individual nations is necessarily always present here, indeed in superfluity . . . the port of Rome [Ostia] is the common marketplace of all people and the common market for the products of the whole earth" (Füssel and Segbers 1995, 336).

In particular, the market for luxury goods was limitless, and pearls were the prime symbol of luxury. The rich were happy to show off those they possessed. It was said that some women had entire landed estates hanging on their earlobes (Seneca, *De Beneficiis* VII, 9, 4). Cleopatra's two precious pearls were world famous (Pliny, *Nat. Hist.* 9, 119), and Lollia Paulina, the wife of the emperor Caligula, was supposed to have owned pearl ornaments valued at forty million sesterces (Pliny, *Nat. Hist.* 9, 117). That would have been the equivalent of ten million denarii, in other words ten million workdays for day laborers. Given an average annual wage of two hundred denarii, this means that fifty thousand day laborers would each have had to work a year to earn that much. But before these luxury goods crossed the counter, countless merchants had to cover long distances by sea and by land to bring

59

together the products of distant countries. The book of Revelation (18:11-19) also reports how these exotic treasures were traded in Rome, but that author views the scene with disgust, as the sign of a city that, through its system of trade and consumption, is being destroyed by its own exploitation. In Rev 17:5 the city of Rome acquires a name drawn from tradition: Babylon. Jewish people, at any rate, knew what that meant. It offered sufficient latitude that other cities could have been meant by it: Alexandria perhaps, Corinth, Antioch. . . .

But for the moment let us return to Rome. In the Via Sacra, near the temple of Romulus, an ancient shop sign has been uncovered. It belonged to a pearl dealer, a *margaritarius*. He was not the only representative of his profession. Countless of his colleagues also had their shops in this thoroughfare of magnificence, where they marketed their pearls and pearl products. From tomb inscriptions we learn that in the Via Sacra alone there were at least seven pearl dealers (*CIL* VI, 9545-9549, 33872; X, 6492). In order to obtain these precious globes the *margaritarii* had to have contacts as far away as the Red Sea, the Persian Gulf, and even the Indian Ocean. They were indebted to Alexander the Great (356–323 B.C.E.) for having opened these commercial routes to the East for them. Many ancient writers, including Pliny the Elder (23/24–79 C.E.), were impressed and wrote extensive accounts of the importance of the pearl trade in their own time (Pliny, *Nat. Hist.* VI, IX).

In contrast, the New Testament is extraordinarily reticent on the subject, which is remarkable in light of the importance of this branch of commerce. Besides the passage in Revelation already mentioned (cf. Rev 17:1-6; 18:11-19) we find reflection of this situation only in the parable of the merchant seeking fine pearls (Matt 13:45-46). The merchant dealing in pearls, however, in contrast to Revelation 18, is here regarded positively, and also has a positive relationship to the reign of God.

Whereas Latin had a proper name for this profession (*margaritarii* are people who deal in *margaritae*, pearls), the merchant in Matt 13:45-46 is presented under the general term *emporōs*, wholesaler. Greek distinguished only between the *emporōs* or wholesaler and the *kapelōs* or retailer (cf. Plato, *Rep.* 2p 371 D). In the first place the terms convey, in their very grammatical form, an impression that only men worked in these professions. As we know, this primarily expresses androcentric perceptions and not necessarily the real social situation in the New Testament period. Hence we are not surprised to learn that, despite abundant evidence of women as merchants in this field in antiquity, we find scarcely anything written about them. But we must suppose that numerous women merchants also moved about, earning their living and making a profit. Since women's wages in this period were not sufficient to secure a minimum subsistence (Schottroff 1995, 94–96), it was probably an attractive option for women to earn their money in trade, despite the risks and dangers involved. When they bought and sold pearls they journeyed far beyond the borders of the Roman empire. These women crossed boundaries, indeed, in a geographical sense as well, when they traveled to India.

But what kind of concrete picture should we make for ourselves of these border-crossing women? A tomb inscription from Rome gave me the clue. Here we make the acquaintance of one such woman: *Domitia, freedwoman of Gnaeus, pearl dealer* (CIL VI, 5972).

We learn nothing more about her, but in view of the many nameless people who have disappeared somewhere, in mass graves, without leaving a trace, this in itself is a great deal. We at least know her name, her social status, and her profession. On the basis of this information we can consider other possibilities. We may presume that this former slave was active as a pearl dealer even before she was freed, and that after that she still remained obligated to her patron in a permanent economic dependency. Surely her work included not only mercantile, but also craft activities, for example goldsmithing, by which she worked the pearls into jewelry, and repairs to the same kinds of objects. It is easy to suppose that Domitia worked alongside a number of other people, since that was the custom for many others in her line of work. Another inscription (*CIL* VI, 5, 3405) introduces us to one of Domitia's colleagues, a woman named Marcia. The inscription was found in Rome, in the inner courtyard of a house near the church of Jesus and Mary: *Marcia Severa, daughter of Titus, goldsmith and pearl dealer in the Via Sacra, has with the testamentary letter endowed (by testament?) her male and female freedpersons and their children.*

The freeborn Roman Marcia was the patron of freedpersons who probably were active in the jewelry business along with their mistress. She apparently established a fund for them. We may therefore assume that Marcia was wealthy, which is not necessarily the case for the pearl dealer Domitia. If the added *columba* on Marcia's tomb inscription means "dove," the symbol could indicate that she was a Christian.

Although the content of this inscription is revealing and yields much information, it is problematic. Unfortunately we do not know if it is genuine, or from what period it comes. However, even if it was made later—perhaps in the Middle Ages—in imitation of ancient models, it can still tell us something. The (almost complete) absence of ancient inscriptions for women who worked as pearl merchants must have been regarded by someone as an omission. By whom? a woman, perhaps? maybe even a fellow pearl merchant, since the inscription reveals some insider knowledge. To whomever we owe this inscription, he or she correctly combined pieces of information about ancient pearl merchants in its content and made use of the possibilities of "historical imagination" (cf. Schüssler Fiorenza 1984, 20), the importance of which has long been recognized in feminist scholarship.

In this way many women are being written back into history, women we normally hear nothing about because patriarchal historiography prevents their being heard. We can only suppose that Domitia and Marcia might have traveled long distances to obtain their precious wares. There were a number of possibilities. Either one bought pearls from traveling merchants who came to Rome, or else one might travel on the customary trade routes to the main transit points (e.g., Alexandria or Palmyra) to meet other merchants, or one could go in person to India to purchase the pearls at the point of origin. Domitia, as a former slave, probably traveled on orders from her patron to carry out his business. Marcia, herself a patron, certainly must have sent out her own traveling employees. There are more legends than realistic descriptions of the situations the merchants found in the different places where the pearls were brought up from the sea. At any rate, in some places prisoners were put to this difficult and dangerous work (*Periplus des Erythräischen Meeres* 59). Many perils lurked beneath the waves: wounds, health-destroying saltwater, sharks. When one considers the massive numbers of pearls that were traded in the Roman empire it is not surprising that, to supply the enormous and steadily increasing demand, people had to be forced to engage in the deathly dangerous job of pearl diving. Had it been possible, the pearl divers would probably have preferred to earn their living in some other way.

Because pearls were easily transported they were also easy to smuggle. This opportunity was certainly pursued with avidity in order to avoid paying the tax collectors. In Quintilian, *Declamationes Minores* 359, there is a description of such a conflict situation. A married woman smuggles four hundred pearls, for which she should rightfully have paid one-fortieth part in customs duty. The conflict arose on the basis of the following regulations: the tax collector was permitted to search travelers, and goods in transport had to be declared. Anything not declared could be forfeit to the tax collector. But he was not permitted to search a married woman. While this woman did not declare the pearls, she offered to let the tax collector search her, which he of course declined. After this the woman produced the pearls, and the tax collector declared that they were forfeit to him. The discussion concerned the action that ought to be taken in this case. The text shows that women, including married women, traveled as pearl dealers. Apparently this was opportune because women in particular could be seen as having pearls for their own use. Under those circumstances it was not easy to determine whether duty was to be paid on them or not. Thus women engaged in mercantile trade benefited from the ideology that says that women like to wear jewelry; disguised as mere consumers, they could travel unmolested across borders.

How, then, was the work of Domitia, Marcia, and the nameless merchant woman regarded in the Christian communities? Did these three perhaps have Christian colleagues? On the basis of the New Testament witness we must suppose that attitudes toward pearl dealers and to trade in general were ambivalent. In Revelation they are among the people who will perish because of their participation in exploitative practices. The attitude of the letter of James (4:13-17; 5:1-6) toward merchants betrays disapproval. This tendency is similar to the thought, expressed earlier in Sir 26:29, that trade is in itself a temptation to wrongdoing. However, the parable in Matt 13:45-46 goes in the opposite direction. Although it contains no application, it is spoken to disciples (Matt 13:36). It can be interpreted as giving a positive evaluation, or at least acceptance, of pearl dealing. In itself it offers no occasion for criticism; what matters is the concrete behavior of the dealer. The attitude of early Christian communities cannot be easily or clearly stated. While Tertullian (*Apol.* 42) takes it as a matter of course that Christian merchants frequented the same marketplaces as other dealers, and so speaks of their working together, the redaction of the Q parable found in Matt 22:1-10//Luke 14:16-24 and in *GThom* 64 can give the impression that merchants were not tolerated in the communities responsible for this tradition, and that at best the reign of God would remain closed to them.

In our attempt to imagine the lives of Christian women merchants we have as starting points only the stories about Lydia, the purple-seller (Acts 16:4), and Priscilla, the tentmaker (Acts 18:3). The mobility and commercial activity of these women must furnish the frame of reference for pearl dealers as well. Trade routes were also mission routes. Merchants were not only on the move for the purpose of buying and selling their wares; religious messages were also spread in the same way. Josephus, *Ant.* 20.17ff., speaks of a Jewish merchant who gave instruction in Judaism to Queen Helena of Adiabene at the court in Charax Spasini on the Persian Gulf, when she was living there in exile with her son.

We should imagine the activity of Christian merchants in similar fashion. In Rom 16:1-2 Paul asks the addressees to support Phoebe, who exercised leadership in the congregation of her home town of Cenchreae, in her business ventures. He does not mention what kind of business this was, but apart from generalized "tasks" his language can also denote "mercantile enterprise," for Phoebe was certainly not traveling merely for her own pleasure. She, too, had to earn her living, and in Cenchreae, one of the port towns attached to Corinth, trade was a principal source of income.

Christian women merchants probably traveled beyond the borders of the Roman empire. In the Acts of Thomas (*ATh* 2) it is presumed that Christian slaves, both female and male, were sold as craftspersons as far away as India. The missionary couples Tryphaena and Tryphosa (Rom 16:12) and Evodia and Syntyche (Phil 4:2), whose professions we do not know, could of course have been merchants. We can no longer learn whether they ever dealt in pearls. The sole trace that can lead us to Christian women as pearl dealers is the tomb inscription of the Roman goldsmith Marcia. She quite certainly had women colleagues who also worked for the spread of the gospel, and to whom the communities therefore were greatly indebted. In many places these women were quite probably the first Christians, because as merchants they were the first to dare to cross borders.

Bibliography

I. Ancient Sources

Corpus Inscriptionum Latinarum. Academia litterarum regiae Borussciae Berolini, ed., 1862– . (= *CIL*)

Hennecke, Edgar, and Wilhelm Schneemelcher, eds., *New Testament Apocrypha.* 2 vols. English translation supervised by Robert McL. Wilson. Philadelphia: Westminster, 1963–1966.

Josephus, Flavius. *Jewish Antiquities,* with an English translation by Henry St. John Thackeray. 9 vols. LCL. Cambridge, Mass.: Harvard University Press, 1998.

L. Annaei Senecae De beneficiis libri VII: De clementia libri II, ed. Carl Hosius. Leipzig: Teubner, 1914.

M. Fabii Quintiliani Declamationes Minores, ed. D. R. Shackleton Bailey. Stuttgart: Teubner, 1989.

Periplus maris Erythraei. Der Periplus des Erythräischen Meeres von einem Unbekannten. Greek and German text by B. Fabricius. Leipzig: Veit, 1883. English: *The Periplus of the Erythraean Sea: Travel and Trade in the Indian Ocean,* by a merchant of the first century. Translated from the Greek and annotated by Wilfred H. Schoff. Philadelphia: Commercial Museum, 1911.

Plato. *The Republic,* with an English translation by Paul Shorey. 2 vols. LCL. Revised ed. London: Heinemann, 1930–1932.

Pliny the Elder. *Natural History,* with an English Translation by H. Rackham. 10 vols. LCL. Cambridge, Mass.: Harvard University Press, 1961.

Tertullian. *Opera.* Turnhout: Brepols, 1954.

II. Modern Sources

Füssel, Kuno, and Franz Segbers, eds. ". . . *so lernen die Völker des Erdkreises Gerechtigkeit. Ein Arbeitsbuch zu Bibel und Ökonomie.* Luzern: Exodus; Salzburg: Pustet, 1995.

Gummerus, Herman. "Die römische Industrie," chs. 1 and 2, *Klio* 14 (1915) 129–89.

_____. "Die römische Industrie," ch. 3, *Klio* 15 (1918) 256–302.

Schottroff, Luise. *Lydia's Impatient Sisters: A Feminist Social History of Early Christianity.* Translated by Barbara and Martin Rumscheidt. Louisville: Westminster John Knox, 1995.

Schüssler Fiorenza, Elisabeth. *Bread Not Stone: The Challenge of Feminist Biblical Interpretation.* Boston: Beacon, 1984.

Warmington, E. H. *The Commerce Between the Roman Empire and India.* 2nd rev. and enlarged ed. London: Curzon; New York: Octagon, 1974.

Luzia Sutter Rehmann

The *Agunah,* the Bound Wife: A Transgressive Woman in Jewish Law and Her Significance for Early Christian Communities

Many years ago the women's movement was interested in witches: Hagazussa, the fence rider, who can make her way along the border between inside and outside, fascinated historians, sociologists, theologians, and all manner of literati. I, too, was attracted by the herb-witches, shaken by the tortured women and girls, and inspired by the phenomenon of thinking everything anew—from the fence, which only appears to hold together the supposedly secure world.

This fascination has since borne fruit. The hagazussa and her muttering have not been driven from the fence, nor is the world free of fences, but the borders have become more permeable, my ears and eyes sharper for fencelike constructions, for borderline phenomena with central significance. I know that many feminist-schooled women scholars no longer allow themselves to be cowed by the fence. The space beyond the fence becomes central when we do not blindly accept the prescribed rules about "inside" and "outside," "important" and "marginal," etcetera. But in exploring that space many of us have become transgressors, joining fields that long were regarded as irreconcilable opposites, moving back and forth between ways of being; we need a lot of energy to keep the points of friction intact.

In Luise Schottroff's doctoral seminar I saw how exciting it is to cross boundaries, opening "borderlands," categories, disciplines, subjects, in order to learn from one another and not to remain fence-sitters in the sense of border guards. For me, the simple question about the life situation of ordinary women and men repeatedly caused the fences to sway. Bringing together facts from the most diverse fields served not to reinforce definitions, but rather to sketch a life context. It is in this sense that I want to present here my reflections on the *agunah.*

Wives changed . . .

Sympathy with a Christian community brought a married woman into difficulties if her husband did not share her enthusiasm. In the oldest apocryphal Acts of Apostles we find not only chastity stories (cf. Burrus 1986, 101) about a great many women, but also marital conflicts brought about by the individual conversions of women (cf. Schottroff 1996, 235).

Tertullian was also aware of the difficulties that the conversion of a wife to Christianity brought with it (*Uxor.* II, 4). He lists all manner of them: when she wants to make a day of reflection, her husband requires her to go with him to the public baths; when she wants to fast, he orders a feast. What husband would permit his wife to rush across the city to visit brothers (!) and sisters? Who would enjoy permitting her to go to night meetings, and at Easter to spend the whole night away from home, or to kiss the chains of the martyrs as they lie in prison? And if nothing else, it is certainly problematic when she goes to a brother, kisses him, and washes his feet.

The apocryphal Acts of Apostles (written ca. 160–200 C.E.) underscore this Church Father's concerns: violent attacks are staged by alarmed husbands, marital conflicts drive women out of their houses and marriages, and the abandoned husbands, fiancés, or mothers bring action in the courts. They often succeed in accusing the apostle as the seducer of the rebellious woman, and even in having him executed.

Let us consider the case of a wife who became a Christian and so entered a severe marital crisis, as Ptolemy and Lucius's *Acts of the Christian Martyrs* describes:

> There was a woman married to a man of evil life, in which she too had formerly participated. But once she had come to know the teachings of Christ she became reformed and tried in turn to persuade her husband to reform his own life. . . . But the man persisted in his licentiousness and alienated his wife by his actions. His wife then thought it would be wrong to continue to live with a man who sought his pleasures from any source whatsoever, no matter whether it was against justice or the natural law; and so she wished to have a divorce. Her relatives, however, earnestly entreated her, advising her to remain, on the ground that her husband might one day attain the hope of amendment, and so she forced herself to stay on with him.
>
> Her husband then departed for Alexandria, and word was brought back that he was behaving worse than before. And so his wife, not wishing to become an accomplice in his crimes and injustices by remaining in wedlock with him, sharing bed and board, gave him

what you call the *repudium* [see the glossary at the end of this article] and left him.

    Now her excellent spouse . . . filed a complaint against her on the ground that she had left him without his consent . . . .
(Musurillo 1972, 39)

This wife's conversion had changed her, so that a common life seemed impossible to her. She saw it as offensive to the teachings of Christ, the righteousness of God. Although her relatives put pressure on her, in the long run she could not continue to live contrary to her convictions. No ascetic motives on the part of the wife are mentioned, but only a deep alienation that made her whole life with her husband impossible. When he went away she made use of the opportunity to prepare a *repudium* and left. The fact that this apparently legal measure could meet with resistance and was subjected to legal challenge is evident from the rest of the story. She was brought before the public officials because her husband was not willing simply to let his wife leave. Either because he had paid no attention before this to her alienation, because he loved her in his own way, or because he did not want to concede her any financial means—in any case, he challenged her behavior.

. . . and left their homes.

    Wives who changed under the influence of the Christian communities could be subjected to enormous pressures. Relatives, husbands, or, as we see in Tertullian's writings, even Christian teachers warned them against making changes that would endanger their marriages. Added to these great spiritual and mental burdens were judicial difficulties, since there were frequently husbands who simply refused to permit a legal divorce. As we saw in the case of the anonymous wife in the *Acts of the Christian Martyrs,* the wife could enter a *repudium,* but it could be challenged by her husband.

    The difficulties seem to have been even greater for a woman living in a Jewish marriage if she did not possess a marriage contract that explicitly stated her right to a divorce on her own initiative. Numerous husbands refused their rebellious wives the *get* [see glossary] or legal divorce. If divorced without a *get* the wife could not engage in any legal procedures: without a *get* no Jewish remarriage was possible, nor could any financial support be demanded. A woman thus separated and rejected was in danger of being an *agunah,* a bound wife, for the rest of her life. Other women, however, left their families, houses, and husbands in search of God. They, too, could easily become *agunoth.* We find some enlightening material on their situation in the Mishnah.

Agunah: **the bound wife**

As long as a Jewish marriage lasted, the woman had the legal status of wife. Marriage ended with death, and the surviving wife became a widow. If she had no children the levirate laws applied, that is, she became *yebamah* (Deut 25:5). Of course, marriage could also end in divorce (Deut 24:1-4). In that case the wife must be given a *get* in her own name. She had to be able to show such a *get,* made out in her own name, in order to retrieve the sum of money prescribed in her *ketubah* contract from her husband or his family. This was her "life insurance," her financial support on which to build a new life. Thus after marriage a wife could undergo a change of status to widow, *yebamah,* or divorcee. But if her husband disappeared, went missing, or gave her no legal *get,* for whatever reasons, the woman became an *agunah,* a "living widow" (Lewittes 1994, 181). David M. Feldman defines the *agunah* as follows: "An *agunah* is a woman who cannot remarry until the death of her missing husband is clearly established or her disputed divorce document is declared legal" (Feldman 1968, 44).

Rachel Biale (1995, 102) lists the following reasons why a woman might become a bound wife:

- The husband leaves his wife and disappears.

- The husband dies but there is no valid witness to his death.

- The marriage has become unendurable, but the husband refuses to agree to a divorce in spite of the efforts of the *beth din* (the Jewish court).

- The marriage has become unendurable, but the husband is legally incapable of agreeing to a divorce (ordinarily because of mental illness).

- A woman becomes *yebamah,* but the *levir* [see glossary] refuses to contract a marriage with her or to carry out the *chalizah* [see glossary], or he cannot be found or is no longer a Jew.

A number of questions arise at this point. As we have seen, an *agunah* could also be a woman who had left her husband on her own initiative without a letter of divorce, or one who was unable to obtain a legal divorce because of her husband's resistance. I am not at all interested in apportioning guilt, nor am I interested in the old and pressing question whether Jewish wives could initiate divorce (Brooten 1982). At this point it is not my intention to enter into the whole complex discussion of Jewish women's right to divorce; my sole question is this: What could a wife do in order not to become *agunah*? What could an *agunah* do to improve her legally and financially unsatisfactory situation?

If he was in conflict with his wife, a husband could refuse to give her a *get*, for example if he did not want her to be able to remarry. In *m. Giṭ* we see how the rabbis discussed the validity of a *get*. A *get* once written and handed over could not be annulled afterward. Apparently this was a point at which a roadblock had to be set up to stop something that had a tendency to happen! Otherwise it would have been very easy to send a wife away and, when there was need of her, to haul her back, or, as soon as another man showed interest in her, to halt that development by stating that the *get* was not valid, had not been rightly conveyed, etc. The rabbis' work toward a uniform *get* formula can readily be understood as a restriction on males' arbitrary behavior (cf. Hauptman, 1998).

But what could an unhappy wife do if her husband was not willing to give her a *get*? What could the *beth din* do for her? Was it possible to compel a divorce against the husband's will?

Forced divorce

When a husband had disappeared and there was no witness to his death there was no way for a wife to obtain permission for a new marriage. She remained bound. In contrast, the Jewish court became an important body for women who wanted to demand a letter of divorce *sub judice* if a husband did not perform his marital duties and would not give her a *get*. In *m. Giṭ* 9,8 it is expressly stated that a forced *get* is valid if it is demanded by a Jewish court. A letter of divorce compelled by a non-Jewish court is only valid if the non-Jews say: "Do what the Israelites tell you!" Thus if the husband is obligated by Jewish law to permit himself to be divorced from his wife, a non-Jewish court can also intervene to bring about the divorce.

There is an interesting example of this in the Jewish papyri from Egypt (cf. Tcherikover 1957, 36). Around 218 B.C.E. Helladote sued for her rights before a Greek, non-Jewish court. She emphasized that her husband Jonathas had married her according to Jewish law; however, he was now holding back one hundred drachmas and their house. This was evidently a matter of marital discord. Jonathas seems to have driven Helladote out of the house. According to her, he had locked her out. I suspect that he had thrown her out without anticipating that she would sue for her rights. But Helladote went to the nearest court and presented her case. She counted off: He did not give her what belonged to her. He locked her out of her own house. He did her injustice "in every respect." The threefold listing recalls *m. Ketub.* 5.6-9. It appears that Jonathas had done wrong on all three levels of marital duty: He did not care for his wife's material needs, he refused her a roof over her head, and he withdrew from his sexual obligations. Helladote does not mention a *get*. It may be that she had none. In that case she would sue for the rectification of the situation to which she was entitled in order not to get into the state of an *agunah*. Her reference to Jewish law makes it clear that under that law she was entitled to certain rights including, for example, the right to a legal divorce.

Why did Helladote not go to a Jewish court? She may have chosen not to do so if, for example, she herself was not Jewish. However, she shows that an appeal to a non-Jewish court could be a matter of course. The accusing party could obviously seek out the court before which her chances would be best. It is interesting, nevertheless, that Helladote asks the non-Jewish court to send a messenger to Samaria: "I beg you therefore, my king, to order Diophanes, the *strategos*, to write to . . . the *epistates* of Samareia not to let . . . to send Jonathas to Diophanes in order . . ." (document is damaged).

Helladote was well informed. Her statement that her marriage to Jonathas was based on Jewish law was necessary so that the non-Jewish court would understand what she was asking of it. She wanted to cause the court to bring the overseer (rabbi) of Samaria into the case in order to force her husband to appear before the court! The non-Jewish court evidently could not simply compel the resistant husband to divorce. But by judicial process it could call on the Jewish court in Samaria to act. This would in effect be equivalent to an authorization: the non-Jewish court could be empowered by the Jewish court in Samaria to give judgment for Helladote against Jonathas (*m. Giṭ* 9,8).

A vengeful husband could force his wife into the situation of an *agunah*, but he himself could marry again without offending against religious law, since in principle polygamy on the part of men was not an offense against the law. An *agunah*, on the other hand, would become an adulteress if she married again, and her children would be *mamserim*, that is, they would be considered illegitimate and not Jewish.

In the Geonic period the rabbinic courts seem to have accommodated themselves more fully to the pressure of women seeking divorce. Apparently there were many women who were going to non-Jewish courts for divorces. That caused the rabbis to change their attitude, for they understood that a rigid interpretation of the law would drive many Jewish women (*agunoth*) to the Gentiles or into prostitution (*b. Giṭ* 88b; Riskin 1989, 135). Judith Hauptman (1998) also refers to this Geonic rule as an indication that Jewish women were appealing to Gentile courts. However, she supposes that the Babylonian as well as the Palestinian discussion in the Mishnah creates the impression that forced divorce was already under discussion in the Amoraic period (ca. 300).

The Talmud specifies as good grounds for seeking a divorce:

- when the husband has physical deformities or damage that the wife can no longer endure (*m. Ketub.* 7.10);

- when the husband neglects his marital duties (shelter, nourishment, clothing) (*m. Ketub.* 5.5-6);

- when there is sexual incompatibility between husband and wife (*m. Ned.* 11.12; *m. Ketub.* 5.7).

We cannot clearly determine whether Jewish courts took a positive or negative attitude toward these grounds when brought by women. Although the Mishnah regards a forced divorce as legitimate, it leaves it to the teachers to seek solutions in concrete cases. But if, according to *m. Ketub.* 7.10, a husband could be forced to divorce because he smelled bad, he could certainly have been compelled to it if he did not provide for his wife's support (*p. Git* 9.9, 50d).

Conclusion and questions

In describing the history of early Christian women we must speak not only of virgins, married women, divorcees, and widows, but also of the transgressive woman *par excellence,* the *agunah.* She is a woman out of line in Jewish law even today, a too-often overlooked marginal figure who cannot enter a new marriage under Jewish law and must live without material security. In law she is a wife, but in fact she lives as "unmarried," "ascetic," "autonomous"—however we want to describe her. She takes quite a lot upon herself. But there are ways for her to compel a divorce before a non-Jewish or Jewish court if she has "good" reasons and her husband can be brought to the bar.

As long as the early communities lived according to the Jewish way of life and Torah it must have been important whether a woman was living in an *agunah* situation or not. As a bound wife she could not in any case consider remarriage without offending against the Torah. I wonder what the *agunoth* in the Christian communities contributed to the construction of the privilege of being free of marriage. It seems to me that the *agunah* teaches us to distinguish better between being separated and divorced, as well as between "freedom from marriage" (Sutter Rehmann 1994) as a chosen way of life and as a necessary situation imposed by law. The *agunah* also makes it clear how important the gender-specific questions surrounding marriage, divorce, remarriage, and freedom from marriage are. For until we acknowledge the legal and religious laws with their inequalities and the resulting different material situations of wives and husbands we have no basis at all for judging the state of the unmarried, and we are in danger of an over-hasty romanticization of it.

Only after considering that can we begin to ask how Paul and the voices in the gospels dealt with the needs of the *agunah,* and whether they succeeded in giving their situation an eschatological reevaluation. Was it a privilege to be accepted into the Christian community as a "runaway" wife, and not to be required to remarry? Or were there women who refused legal confrontations in order not to damage the Christian movement, and thus "freely" remained *agunah?* How did *agunoth* who had become Christian interpret themselves—as wives who were materially dependent on the community and enslaved by the marriage laws? Or did they, despite the one-sided marriage laws, discover niches in the new community out of which utopias could sprout?

Glossary

Chalizah is explained as "removal of a shoe." The act is described in detail in *m. Yeb.* 12.6. If a *levir* cannot marry his brother's widow he must take off his shoe and declare his will before the court.

Geonim were the leading teachers in numerous Babylonian academies between 700 and 1000. Their discussions are found in the Babylonian Talmud.

Get: The principal part of the letter of divorce consists of a clear declaration that the wife is from now on free to marry if she so desires. See *m. Giṭ* 9.3: "You are now a free woman; you belong to yourself." This statement must be signed by the husband and the witnesses.

Levir is the one who must beget a male heir for a dead man, and who therefore must marry his widow. The degrees of relationship determine which of the dead man's family is to be *levir.*

Repudium is a declaration by one party to an agreement that the contract is annulled. The concept is also used in divorce practice either for an oral declaration before witnesses, a letter, or the declaration of a messenger to the other party. Such a declaration must be followed by the termination of common life. A *repudium ex justa causa* brought with it financial costs (the loss of the dowry or marriage presents) for the party whose bad behavior legitimated the divorce. On this see Adolf Berger, *Encyclopedic Dictionary of Roman Law* (Philadelphia: American Philosophical Society, 1953) 676.

Bibliography

Biale, Rachel. *Women and Jewish Law. The Essential Texts, Their History, and Their Relevance for Today.* 2nd revised ed. New York: Schocken, 1995.

Brooten, Bernadette J. "Konnten Frauen im alten Judentum die Scheidung betreiben? Überlegungen zu Mk 10,11-12 und 1 Kor 7,10-11," *EvTh* 42 (1982) 65–80. For responses see the articles by Eduard Schweizer, *EvTh* 42 (1982) 294–300, and Hans Weder, *EvTh* 43 (1983) 466–78.

Burrus, Virginia. "Chastity as Autonomy: Women in the Stories of the Apocryphal Acts," *Semeia* 38 (1986) 101–17.

Feldman, David M. *Birth Control in Jewish Law; Marital Relations, Contraception, and Abortion as Set Forth in the Classic Texts of Jewish Law.* New York: New York University Press, 1968.

Hauptman, Judith. *Rereading the Rabbis: A Woman's Voice.* Boulder, Colo.: Westview, 1998.

Hennecke, Edgar, and Wilhelm Schneemelcher, eds., *New Testament Apocrypha.* 2 vols. English translation supervised by Robert McL. Wilson. Philadelphia: Westminster, 1963–1966.

Lewittes, Mendell. *Jewish Marriage: Rabbinic Law, Legend, and Custom.* Northvale, N.J.: Jason Aronson, 1994.

Musurillo, Herbert. *The Acts of the Christian Martyrs.* Oxford: Clarendon Press, 1972.

Riskin, Shlomo. *Women and Jewish Divorce: The Rebellious Wife, the Agunah, and the Right of Women to Initiate Divorce in Jewish Law. A Halakhic Solution.* Hoboken, N.J.: Ktav, 1989.

Schottroff, Luise. "'Gesetzesfreies Heidenchristentum'—und die Frauen? Feministische Analysen und Alternativen," in Luise Schottroff and Marie-Theres Wacker, eds., *Von der Wurzel getragen. Christlich-feministische Exegese in Auseinandersetzung mit Antijudaismus.* Leiden and New York: Brill, 1996, 227–45.

Sutter Rehmann, Luzia. "'Und ihr werdet ohne Sorge sein. . . .' Gedanken zum Phänomen der Ehefreiheit im frühen Christentun," in Dorothee Sölle, ed., *Für Gerechtigkeit streiten: Theologie im Alltag einer bedrohten Welt.* Gütersloh: Chr. Kaiser, 1994, 88–95.

Tcherikover, Anat. *Corpus Papyrorum Judaicarum* I. Cambridge: Harvard University Press, 1957.

Tertullian. *Ad uxorem,* in Charles Nunier, editor and translator, *A son Epouse.* SC 273. Paris: Cerf, 1980.

Wasserstein, Abraham. "A Marriage Contract from the Province of Arabia Nova: Notes on Papyrus Yadin 18," *Jewish Quarterly Review* 80 (1989) 93–130.

Sigrun Wetzlaugk

"Do Justice for Me!"

Dear Luise, dear transgressor-women,

I am one of the widows from the port city of Joppa in Judea who lived and worked in community with Tabitha. You read about us in Acts 9:36-42.

With much curiosity we heard about your project on "transgressors." When we women sew together, sometimes deep into the night, we talk about questions that interest us. "Transgressors"—the word itself rouses many questions and thoughts in us; after all, there are boundaries enough in our lives:

- the death of a husband as the boundary of his life and of our life together;

- the boundaries set against us because of our widowhood;

- the limits set on our opportunities to shape our own lives;

- the narrowly defined boundaries within which we can earn our very livelihood through hard work;

- the frequent boundary violations and attacks that we experience and suffer;

- and finally the confrontation with our own limitations, the boundaries of our abilities and possibilities, our strength and endurance.

Cut off, fenced in, forced to the margins, wounded, exploited, ignored—all these experiences are contained, for us, in that word "boundaries." But then there are all the wholesome and protective aspects of boundaries: setting myself apart, being able to set clear boundaries. In our tradition there are very important, indispensable boundaries set by God that serve life, limit suffering and misery, set bounds to arbitrariness and injustice, boundaries that are meant to protect us widows, too.

The longer we reflect on the boundary experiences in our life, the more important is the emphasis on "going," on activity. We are not passive; we not only confront barriers, suffer them, but deal with them, rub against them, change and cross boundaries that shut us out; we defend ourselves against boundary violations and we set boundaries.

We have heard that many of you have learned, through your work, Luise, to love the parable of the stubborn widow (Luke 18:1-8) as "a little story of women's resistance to injustice." We are very happy about that, for the story is very important in our community, and not only for us widows. It is part of the oral tradition of the Jesus movement that we tell each other in our houses and community gatherings and hand on to others as part of our Jewish tradition. Of course, in all our conversations and discussions in the community we draw on the religious treasure of our people. I say this explicitly because in the commentaries from your own time the traditions that are so important to us have often become invisible.

I still remember vividly the day when I heard the story of the stubborn widow for the first time. As you know from reading about the Jerusalem community in the Acts of the Apostles (Acts 2:42-47), we also meet every evening for a common meal and prayers in one of our houses. This common daily eating and drinking, the sharing of bread so that all are filled, is inseparably linked with our hope for the reign of God, which will bring justice. Common prayer and shared bread are part of our praxis of justice and resistance. In these daily gatherings we pray, read the Scriptures together and interpret them; sometimes we pass on the oral traditions, and sometimes we argue about our praxis. On one of those evenings the disciple Tabitha told us the story of the widow, and since then it has really been part of me. Since that day we recall, day by day as we weave and sew garments together, the story of that woman who fought for her rights. It is our story of hope against resignation. That is Gospel for us: a widow obtains her rights after a long wait. The power of injustice is briefly interrupted. What seemed impossible becomes possible: a widow fights an unjust judge and wins her rights. It is a story that expresses and keeps alive our longing and our cry for justice.

In our community I learned a new perspective on my own life from this widow who goes to court and tirelessly demands her rights. Until then my outlook had always been shaped by self-surrender and care for others. Demanding something—that was only for others, for the weaker members, for my children, for my old parents. I never learned to ask something for myself, to claim my own rights. I felt that very painfully after my husband's death. I was an easy victim of boundary violations. I had never learned to defend myself, to speak out. In fact,

I had always worked in secret. Certainly I fought for my ideas; I was no conformist. I had accomplished quite a lot, but seldom through open confrontation, more in secret, at the level of relationships. I had to learn how to say: I have rights and if necessary I will take you to court to obtain them. Before my husband's death that idea was entirely foreign to me. In fact, I had to learn what my rights were, since as a wife I had nothing to do with the courts; my husband took care of legal matters and I had scarcely any notion of the law. The idea of standing before the court made me terribly anxious. How would I appear before the court? What would I appeal to? How would I express myself? How would the people around me react, how would my opponent in the suit react? Today I know that I often used to invest all my strength in enduring unjust situations, not in changing them. I tried to resolve conflicts in the private sphere instead of demanding my rights, and I was astounded to hear that the same is often true even among you.

I have come to treasure the story of the widow fighting for her rights. That woman has become my sister, one who shows me a completely different way: She knows her rights, she goes out in public, stands before the court and demands: "Do justice for me against my opponent!" From this sister of mine I learned to say: "Do justice for me!"—very softly at first, but later with a strong and determined voice: "Do justice for me!"

How often do we widows experience injustice in our lives! How hard and often hopeless it is for us to defend ourselves against it! How many humiliations and disappointments have a lot of us experienced, without obtaining justice! Even though we are touched by injustice to different degrees, we can all sing the song of injustice great and small. Injustice toward widows is shockingly normal. That in itself is dangerous: injustice is so ordinary and everyday that it is scarcely noticed. Nobody even talks about it. For me, that is a very important aspect: bringing injustice out in the open, talking about it.

Even when I heard the story for the first time the injustice that the "opponent" had done to the widow was not concretely named. I still remember that I was very angry at that. We are telling ourselves a story that encourages us to make injustice public, and then she doesn't even say what it is. I wanted to know what it was. Who is this "opponent"? What kind of injustice was it? I wanted to know the woman's story, be able to call her by name. I wanted to know how old she was, how she lived and what she lived on, who her husband was and how he died. It made me angry that the tradition was silent about that, because it seemed so typical: after the first period of mourning, the silence comes very quickly. No one asks you about your story any more; scarcely anyone even mentions your husband's name; hardly anyone really wants to know how you're getting along. It is as though that one word "widow" told the whole story!

When I blurted all that out, everyone looked at me with shocked faces. Suddenly I was the center of attention. "Tell us about your experience!" said Tabitha in the silence that followed. Stuttering, I began to tell, because I had internalized the idea that my suffering was of no interest to anyone—except for God and a few people close to me. Now we were no longer talking about the widow in the parable and our ideas about her, but about me and every other widow in our community, the injustice we suffer and the struggles we carry out, our hopes, our sources of strength.

Today, when we preach the parable of the widow we name our opponents: creditors, tax collectors, landlords, thieves, soldiers of the occupation, and often enough our neighbors and family members, even our own sons. We tell of the injustice we ourselves have suffered: the refusal of our right to clothing, food, and housing that our *ketubah*, our marriage contracts guarantee to us—if we are lucky—the merciless collection of debts and taxes, mortgaging ourselves to the last shirt, being driven out of house and property, the theft of our cattle and our meager belongings, the seizure of our land and acreage when boundaries are shifted, the refusal of payments owed to us, subtle pressures, threats, and violence that take the last bits of what we have, humiliation and degradation when we look for someone to help and protect us.

What strikes almost all of us, and what we cannot legally withstand, is that in spite of our hard work our wages are not adequate for survival, that we go on and on in misery because we earn only a fraction of what men receive for the same work—and even their wages as a rule are not sufficient for a family. The poor economic situation forces many of us to work harder and harder while becoming poorer and sicker, accepting more and more humiliations and acceding to bad work offers or marriage proposals.

As we gradually told of our experiences it became very clear that we dealt with injustice in very different ways. With horror we discovered that we often acted quite differently from the resistant widow, that our reality was more frequently marked by apathy, silence, quiet suffering, and concern for daily survival. A long lawsuit and many trips to the responsible authorities cost a lot of time and strength—strength that we need for the struggle to survive. In our circumstances we cannot afford long proceedings before the law. Add to that the poor prospects of obtaining justice and the fear of getting into still greater danger. We are afraid of legal dealings and more violence. Too often we have heard and seen how inconvenient whistleblowers who bring the truth to light are silenced with threats, violence, and murder. For the judge whom the stubborn widow opposed is not unique: the psalms and the prophetic accusations against the denial or twisting of justice, lies, false witness, and bribery speak very clearly. Injustice and the absence of any fear of God are two sides of the same coin.

It is clear to us that the widow in Luke 18:1-8 knows what kind of judge she is dealing with, for we also know what the judges in our city are like. She knows that he does not fear God or respect other human beings, that he is unjust. He does not ask about the will of God or God's laws; he feels secure in his self-glorification and does not believe that God sees his deeds and will call him to account. She knows that as a widow she holds a bad hand in this game, that her prospects of obtaining justice before this judge are just about zero. And still she goes to him and demands her rights. Where does she get the courage, the strength? Would we even bother going to such a judge? Wouldn't we instead just be resigned from the start, because the effort is so hopeless? This widow, as we keep telling ourselves, goes to the unjust judge and demands her rights. Then she gets just what was to be expected, and what a lot of people before her had experienced: the judge will not give her justice. He has no respect for her rights; he even doubles the injustice. We know a lot of stories like this about people who have fought in vain for their rights. "For a while he refused" stands for the painful experiences of our sisters and brothers: unheard, turned away, kept waiting, put off, all without anything happening. The widow had to go through that again and again. But she never gives up, and she keeps demanding her rights. How long can anyone endure all that? How long before they are worn down, resigned, broken?—days, weeks, years? Who supports them, who gives them courage? Where do they get their strength? What do they do with their disappointment, their rage, their misery? Who listens to them?

I still remember clearly how one of our sisters began, in the silence, to pray the Psalms—psalms that express those very thoughts: the urgent question, "how long?," the feeling of being handed over and abandoned, of wavering, of breaking, strength dissolving, and still, at the same time, a stubborn clinging to God and a passionate cry: "Do justice for me according to your righteousness!"

When we gather we often pray the Psalms. They are our song book; they give us a language for our misery, for our despair, for our rage and hope. They speak of our experience, that the oppressed seek their rights in vain, that the unjust succeed, the exploiters triumph. These are our songs of resistance against the omnipresent danger of falling silent in the face of this overpowering injustice and violence, of abandoning our rights, our hopes, ourselves. The Psalms opened my eyes to the fact that the exploiters and oppressors are only waiting for me to lose the ground under my feet, waiting until I am at an end, till I fall silent. They let time work for them. When we sing or say the Psalms together we cling fast to our faith in God's justice, lamenting, accusing, and demanding—in the faith that God hears our cry and will lead us, the poor, the widows, the orphans, the strangers, the hungry, out of our misery. Borne by the thousands who pray and have prayed and will pray these texts before us, with us, and after us, we enter into conversation with the psalms and sing and speak them as our own words. I remember times when I was close to breaking, close to despair, and this common praying of the Psalms preserved me from falling dumb. In those times of silence I could let myself be borne by the community's prayer, and at some point I could join in it again. I could borrow words from my people's tradition so that I was once again able to speak, to protest, to accuse, and to demand liberation.

It appears to me that the widow in this parable does exactly the same thing. She stands within the tradition of our people: "Do me justice!" This, the central demand of the widow on the judge, immediately recalls our psalms of lament. She directs this cry for justice from the psalms to God *and* the judge—in public! She criticizes and uncovers a corrupt judicial practice that treads upon the rights of us poor people, and she contrasts that practice with God's dealing, God who is father to the orphans and a judge for the widows (Ps 68:6). But in doing so she goes beyond her own individual case and sets herself in the midst of all those whose rights are ignored. In her action, prayer and resistance are joined.

When our courage fails, when helplessness and resignation are spreading, we can draw strength from reminding each other of the story of the widow, and the other stories of widows in our tradition: Tamar, who obtains her rights through trickery, Ruth and Naomi, Judith, who freed her people. We sing the songs of praise of our (fore)sisters who speak of the fall of the violent and the mighty. Before taking difficult steps we will speak to each other in the words of Judith, summoning strength and praying:

> Look at their pride, and send your wrath upon their heads. Give to me, a widow, the strength to resist . . . crush their arrogance by the hand of a woman! For your strength does not depend on influence and money, your rule does not call for great men; you are the God of the lowly, helper of the oppressed, upholder of the weak, protector of the forsaken, savior of those without hope. (Jdt 9:9-11)

We learned to see God in the widow. In her stand for justice she is a parable of God's intervention and of prayer. As in her, so in us and in our actions God can become visible. The parable bears and is borne by our vision that justice begins from below, with the least, the widows, the orphans, the foreigners—with us.

When we heard how our story of the widow, our story of hope and resistance, is read in the popular interpretations of your time we were, to tell you honestly, enraged. The widow is made so tame, so humble, so helpless; her passionate struggle for justice is passed over and not taken seriously. She becomes a supplicant who is unable to do anything but beg. No, indeed, that was not our perspective! This image of the helpless widow fits all too well within the multiple pictures of the powerlessness and subjection of women that are continually held before our eyes and prevent us from encountering violence with resistance and fighting for our rights and our liberation. As poor people, and still more as women, we have so often found that begging gets us no farther, that we are simply not heard unless we are loud and annoying. We see the widow as one who prays, but praying, for us, means not only asking, but shouting, weeping, lamenting, demanding.

That is why we are so happy that you, Luise, have made the resistant widow visible "as a model for the behavior of all believers toward God and other human beings." For us she is important as a woman who knows her rights and claims them, who goes public and does not avoid the law court and repeatedly demands: Do justice for me! She is important as someone deprived of rights, who names injustice for what it is and calls the enemy by name as well. She is important as a stubborn, tireless woman who does not allow herself to be turned away or put off. She is important as a fighter who is not afraid to be annoying and inconvenient, to make trouble. She is important as someone defamed and therefore in danger who is accused, because of her fight for justice, of being dangerous, violent. She is important as one who prays, who names and changes her situation through the language of tradition.

Unlike what many interpreters have tried to make you believe, we understand this tradition not primarily as an injunction to constant prayer. As you know, common prayer has a fixed place in our community and daily life. We understand the parable as a challenge to our actions. Does our praxis match our prayers? Do we offer resistance to unjust structures and people? Do we bring the truth of injustice to light? Is justice something that can be experienced in our community, and in our common life?

In our community we are continually struggling for answers to these questions. The most important thing for us is that our life together should become more and more just. Our daily, common eating and drinking, our sharing of bread and belongings (Acts 2:42-47), and our common prayer—we see all these as a response to the question of justice. Certainly we are not without conflicts; we are not ideal. The argument between the Hellenistic widows at one such daily meal (Acts 6:1) shows that clearly enough. It is painful to demand justice and at the same time to see that some do not want it, even in their own ranks.

Within our community and beyond, we widows have formed a special community of women young and old, wives whose husbands were murdered by the Romans or who died of diseases, women abandoned by their husbands. Through our common work and mutual protection we are working to improve our living conditions and to create for ourselves a place outside the bonds of marriage. By supporting each other in daily questions as well as in the struggle for our rights we are succeeding in overcoming our fear and going out in public to make our situation and the injustice of it better known, to secure our rights, to publicize the infringements of rights practiced by the Roman army, to see to it that our dignity is respected. Along this tedious and difficult path we are borne up by our hope in the God who does justice, who hears our cries. We gather strength from our prayers and celebrate the little "victories" of justice.

We greet you from our hearts, Luise, and with you all your fellow fighters and transgressors. Guard your hope in justice as a precious treasure, for it is terribly fragile in face of the massive force of injustice. Tell each other stories of hope, stories that preserve memories different from those of the victors. Unsuspected strength radiates from those stories. Never surrender your longing and your struggle for justice—for God will do justice for you.

> Let us cry to God: do justice for us!
> Let us pray for ourselves,
> that we will take courage and get up, again and again,
> and stand against the injustice of this world;
> that we will be faithful comrades of God, working for a just world,
> borne by hope and the coming of the Son of Humanity to bring the
> world to its fulfillment.

Shalom.

Bibliography

Richter Reimer, Ivoni. *Women in the Acts of the Apostles: A Feminist Liberation Perspective.* Translated by Linda M. Maloney. Minneapolis: Fortress, 1995.

_____. "Die Macht einer Protagonistin. Das Gebet der Entrechteten (Lk 18, 1-8)." Paper given at the symposium "Ist unser Erbe unsere Macht?" in honor of Luise Schottroff's sixtieth birthday, Hofgeismar, 1994.

Schottroff, Luise. *Lydia's Impatient Sisters: A Feminist Social History of Early Christianity.* Translated by Barbara and Martin Rumscheidt. Louisville: Westminster John Knox, 1995.

_____. "Bodies, Bread, and *basileia:* A Feminist Perspective on the Eschatology of Jesus." Unpublished manuscript.

Schottroff, Willy. "Die Armut der Witwen," in Marlene Crüsemann and Willy Schottroff, eds., *Schuld und Schulden.* Munich: Kaiser, 1992.

Ivoni Richter Reimer

Life Calls for Triumph and Celebration

Ours is an exciting era. We have been talking everywhere of the beginning of a new century that is simultaneously the beginning of a new millennium. Hopes and fears are given religious interpretation, if not exploitation in terms of an apocalyptic period. This is also a time of celebration. Great events are commemorated and expectations are given expression. I am thinking of the five-hundredth anniversary of the "discovery" of Brazil, fifty years since the Declaration of Human Rights, the biblical jubilee: Jubilee 2000! There are different forms of memory work. What interests us here is the critical work of building consciousness, thinking about the content and the strategies of what we are celebrating in terms of eschatological time. We have no interest in celebrating great dates and heroes. We want to celebrate life, which has triumphed and will triumph on the ways of freedom through justice.

This essay was inspired by many suggestions and questions that were expressed in my work with women's groups in Brazil when we discussed human rights and women's rights. My aim is to establish signposts in the form of encouragements and stimuli. Nothing is finished, but much is in process: seeds of the work for the reign of God.

Human Rights and Attacks on the Human Rights of Women in Brazil

Increasingly, even in Brazil, various forms of violence against women are being brought to public notice. The resulting picture is horrifying: it is often the patriarchal household that is the locus of violence against children and women. Violence against women, usually combined with sexual mistreatment and abuse, saturates the whole society. In homes like palaces and in huts made of cardboard, in the country and in the cities of millions, everywhere reality shows the same face: women suffer sexual, physical, and mental violence from (their) men.

A recent investigation of violence against women throughout the nation showed that in Brazil 336 women are beaten, raped, and mistreated in their own houses *every day*. These numbers count only women who have dared to make a public complaint against their attackers. The real mass of acts of violence and experiences of violence is thus much greater. Heleieth Safiotti, a sociologist, determined as early as 1988 that 48.2% of violent acts against women took place within their homes. Women in various human rights organizations attest to this fact: this is a kind of violence that is not intended to kill women, but instead to train them to subordination, passive obedience, and silence.

This assertion is supported by the National Council on the Human Rights of Women, which published a 1998 study entitled *A Primavera já partiu (Spring Is Already Past)*. This study lists the official statistics on the murders of women: each year 2,163 women are murdered (constituting ten percent of the whole number of murder victims). While most murders of men took place on the streets or in public bars, the murders of women mainly occurred in their homes and were done by their own husbands. This is, in fact, a chronic sickness of our society. To oppose it, legal and public health measures must be established and put in place; the need is urgent.

Organizations for human rights and women's rights are working to make this situation known and to denounce violence against women as a violation of their human rights. This work of applying pressure at the base has achieved a hearing before the National Program for Human Rights, and with the aid of organs of the federal government an important change in the laws has been enacted: rape is now regarded in law as a "crime against the person," and no longer, as it was previously, as a "crime against morals." This is progress, in light of the ideas connected with the violence: injuries at the customary and moral level can more easily be excused and tolerated than injuries to the person and its integrity. This change in the laws is important also because it encourages the victims to make complaints without feeling that they themselves are guilty and ought to be ashamed. Signs of solidarity can be addressed more directly to the victims. Women's consciousness regarding violence and its causes is changing.

Are There Points of Orientation in the Bible?

Does the Bible contain points of orientation for questions of violation of the human rights of women? Can women draw words of empowerment and liberation from the subversive memories contained in the Bible when they seek to implement their rights?

These questions should, in the first place, be given a positive answer on the basis of the liberating power that springs from the living word of God. Where there are death-dealing mechanisms at work, whether personal or systematic, it is important to regain definitive, lifegiving biblical witness to the life that is endangered.

In general, we may speak of the indispensable fact that women and men are images of God. This has special theological relevance in women's daily lives. What is the mistreatment of a woman, if it is not to be regarded also as a mistreatment of God? God suffers with the suffering of the mistreated, in the bodies of raped women. God suffers every time a woman is beaten, when any kind of violence is used against women. The body of the woman suffering violence is the word of God in the form of prophetic speech.

Ecclesiologically also, attacks on the human rights of women are central and vitally important. The Body of Christ suffers every time, and again and again, when a woman experiences discrimination and violence. The local and universal *ekklesia* continually suffers damage and loss to its unity when a woman's integrity is damaged, not respected, not honored (see 1 Cor 12:12-31). The familiar, worldwide patriarchal violence against women calls into question the church's authenticity as an organic and solidary society. The bodies of women who suffer violence demand a fully concrete word that will be effective in this situation: a living word. The lives of women imperiled by violence demand the lived and life-supporting word of God.

The Right to Rights and Justice

The issue of human rights, civil rights, and their realization is not just of current interest. It was a central question for women, children, and men in earlier times, including the first century of our era in all the lands and districts conquered and ruled by the Roman empire. The lack of freedom, the dangers experienced through threats, violence, and death caused even Paul to assert that, as far as "civil rights" are concerned, we should direct our eyes to (the kingdom of) heaven, where our liberation in Christ will take place (Phil 3:20-21). For that reason we should behave as citizens according to the Gospel of Jesus Christ, which brings into our lives both righteousness and courage in face of the violent (Phil 1:27-28).

What is true for us today is true also in a certain sense for other ages as well: there are rights that are indispensable, but that do not "function" automatically. They require our dedication, our stubborn commitment, our rage, and our love in order to become reality. But there are also laws and rules, the fruits of different times, cultures, historical and political powers, that are not always applied to the defense of human rights, or that were never brought into effect at all. In short: laws do not always reflect reality, nor do they always effect (human) rights. The same appears to be true for legal texts in biblical times.

Rights and Law in the Lives of Women of the First Century C.E.

In Greco-Roman and Jewish society in the first century by far the majority of widows were marginalized. Judaism emphasized that both women and men were made in the image of God, thus establishing an equality between the sexes. But practically, and in daily life, a woman was for the most part only valued when she lived in a condition of patriarchal dependency on a man, either her father or her husband.

As a result, a woman's ability to exercise her civil rights was restricted, and in most cases even nonexistent. Richer or nobler women exercised some political influence in the life of the city; poorer and working women had political influence within the life and organization of the cooperatives and craft guilds to which they belonged. Their influence was always connected with their function in society, in the guild organization, and then, later, in the church. But that by no means signified that a woman could assert herself, as a woman, in that society.

Consequently some laws existed within Jewish society that applied to married women. To prevent widows from being abandoned and despised, customs and laws were established to protect women, within the conceptions prevalent at the time, from economic need and helplessness. Two laws in particular are of interest in this connection:

The *levirate* laws (cf. Crüsemann 1992, especially 291–303) could be brought into play when a woman was widowed and her marriage had produced no children (or rather, no sons) who could guarantee a continued progeny for the husband and care for the parents in their old age. The law provided that in such a case a brother or other relative of the dead husband should marry the widow. He was then called the widow's *goʾel* (liberator). In patriarchal perspective, the levirate became a right of widows.

The well-known Old Testament story of Ruth (cf. Petermann 1998, 104–13) illustrates how two women succeeded in bringing the levirate into operation. The right was only achieved through the wise initiative of the two women; they illustrate how private rights became public. Undoubtedly there were many widows who remained without a *goʾel*. The right and the law were often not carried into effect, and widows were then marginalized if they could not count on a community of women such as Naomi enjoyed with Ruth. The question remains: what was to be done in order to bring one's rights into effect?

The *ketubah* was a law regarding the marriage contract. When they married, the woman and the man, together with witnesses, signed a marriage contract that, among its many clauses, guaranteed certain important rights of the wife. For example, the husband could not control the whole property alone. For the sale of property he needed the written consent of his wife, attested by witnesses. If she separated from her husband, or if he died, the wife had a claim to a certain sum of money laid down in the contract. The question here again was: how were these rights to be realized?

In all periods of history this is one of the central questions regarding all human and civil rights, and also for initiatives toward their accomplishment. It is expressed in biblical narratives as well; it is meant to encourage us and call us to solidarity. But these stories also call us to a critical engagement with the law itself.

Let me refer to two biblical stories that show us two different forms of laws and two different forms of action for the realization of human rights.

A Woman Fights for Her Own Rights— In Accordance with the Law

Luke 18:1-8 presents us with a parable about prayer in which a widow is protagonist. I understand her to be a protagonist who acts like a citizen, demanding her rights (cf. Richter Reimer 1996; Schottroff 1995, 101–18). The fact that the widow seeks out the judge, and the verb *ekdikēson* ("grant me justice") make it clear that the woman knows her rights and the "legal channels." The widow speaks of her "opponent," who in these circumstances would be her adversary before the law (*antidikos*). The woman behaves in an unusual manner in the framework of what the law envisions—unusual because normally, on the one hand, it is not to be expected, in the context of a patriarchal society, that a woman knows her rights and fights for them, and on the other hand because she does it in an urgent and forceful manner. She goes again and again to the judge, and again and again the judge tries to ignore her and to do nothing for her. He is described literally as a "judge of unrighteousness," who neither feared God nor had respect for people. She makes a lot of trouble for him; that is, she creates a lot of work for him. He is even afraid that ultimately she could hit him in the face. Here we see an example of patriarchal fear of being publicly boxed on the ear by a woman and thus losing face—not because a man has been struck by a woman, but because a judge would have to carry a black mark on him as a sign of his unrighteousness and his refusal to act on behalf of the rights of a widow.

The widow obtains her rights, probably those provided for in the levirate laws or in her *ketubah*. She does it by taking legal steps. She acts "according to the law." But she does not achieve her rights for the sake of right and justice, but because of the judge's fear of losing status. Thus the story of the widow exposes and denounces the hearts of countless judges who, locally and throughout the world, act like this judge of unrighteousness.

In the parable, Jesus is on the side of the widow. He takes her as an example. Her knowledge, her tireless work in the process of achieving her rights, and her stubbornness all serve as examples for the prayer that pleases God. Her story is part of the Bible's subversive memory that gives us courage and enables us to learn our rights and to work over the long haul to achieve them, in order to resist injustice and general passivity.

A Man Advocates for the Rights of a Woman—Against the Law

John 8:1-11 tells of Jesus' liberating action on behalf of a woman who was captured in adultery *(moixeia)*. Scribes and Pharisees brought her to Jesus early in the morning, as he was teaching in the Temple. The woman is put in the center, and Jesus is called upon to give judgment on the woman's action and at the same time on the Law of Moses, which prescribed stoning for such cases.

The Greek text at this point does not quote directly from the Old Testament, but some references are marginally introduced (Lev 20:10 and Deut 22:22-24) to emphasize that in a case of adultery both parties, the man and the woman, are to suffer death. But only in Deut 22:23-24 is stoning prescribed (cf. Crüsemann 1992, who unfortunately does not analyze the case of Deut 22:23-24 in particular). Numbers 5:12-31 is alluded to because of the necessary witnesses, and Deut 17:7 because of the listing in order of those who may stone (in that case on account of idolatry).

The action of the woman is described as adultery. We do not know, however, whether she is a married woman or a woman promised in marriage. She could, in fact, be a *na'arah*, a betrothed virgin, because Deut 22:23-24 refers to such a woman and applies stoning in this case. In addition, stoning is prescribed in the case of a betrothed virgin who, it turns out, is no longer a virgin (Deut 22:20-21). When it is a case of adultery by an *išša* ("wife") and an *iš* ("husband") the text speaks only of capital punishment in general, without describing the type (Deut 22:22)!

Deuteronomy 22:23-24 speaks of the rape of a betrothed virgin *(na'arah)* in the city, and Deut 22:25-27 of the rape of a betrothed virgin *(na'arah)* in an open field. Stoning is prescribed for the former because she did not cry out; nothing is to happen to the latter because "she has not committed an offense punishable by death." She cried out, but there was no one to help her. It is presumed that it is always possible for a raped woman to cry out, that in the city her cry will be heard and someone will come to her aid. Whether in antiquity that was really the case, or only in the minds of the men who wrote the texts, at any rate such presumptions are not valid in our day and age.

If the woman in John 8 is a betrothed virgin to whom Jesus' words in v. 11 apply (see Deut 22:26), we can also speak of *moixeia* as rape. The verb is medial in v. 4 and in this case means "to be seduced into adultery" (Hauck, 737). Thus she is not the subject of the adultery, but has suffered violence. Such a woman is to be stoned (John 8:5) because she did not cry out in the city (Deut 22:23-24). That is probably her "sin" (cf. Deut 22:26), which she should not repeat (John 8:11). A look at these (possible) background circumstances of the scene reveals an action that is not in the first place moral or immoral. We see a woman who suffers violence both in the sex act and afterward, when that same woman is to be judged by a court of men.

Jesus understands this situation and relativizes the law by asking about the sin. Here, as so often, it is a matter of injured life to which still more damage and injustice is to be applied. Unfortunately, he does not ask about the man who, according to the Law, should also be brought forward.

With the time that Jesus gains for us and for himself by writing with his finger on the ground he prevents hasty and "right" answers. There is time for reflection. The letter is not the most important thing, but always the reflection on and for life that lies behind and within it and depends on it. Therefore Jesus can say, "Let anyone among you who is without sin be the first to throw a stone at her." No one condemns her. Jesus sends her off to a new life. She is delivered from the shameful guilt that she suffered because of the violence she had experienced. She was delivered from the wicked tongues, ours included. And yet this painful memory is part of our own memory and of the history of terror and violence against women.

In both stories we find nameless women who, however, are paradigmatic for the life of the communities in solidarity with the despised in the first century. These stories present some important christological and theological aspects:

- Jesus restores the indispensable right of the woman to life and dignity. In doing so, he also calls the lifegiving God (Psalm 82) to life. He corrects a distorted image of God, who reveals Godself not in death—for the sake of patriarchal honor!—but in life.

- God is the life-force who intervenes on behalf of the woman's right. God stands in solidarity on the side of the woman suffering violence, the woman whose life is threatened; in the same way God stands by the woman who fights for her right and does not give up.

- The image of God, God's very self, is liberated by the demand for and defense of the rights of women and is thereby made the center of our lives. Where injustice reigns, God suffers injustice alongside those who suffer.

Consequences

I have not been able to give a full treatment to the subject here. These are only suggestions, words for reflection. Now I want to emphasize two consequences of these stories that are important for my work with women's groups in Brazil, who are dealing with the theme of human rights.

1. Stubbornness, skill in argument, civil courage, coolness, and endurance are words that Jesus applies and affirms, by way of example, in the widow. In doing so he also calls to us and encourages us in naming and accomplishing our human and civil rights. This can be our prayer. Prayer means not giving up; it means that we get underway to bring to reality what we ask of God, the things we most need for a dignified and just life. To do this we must obviously "go public" ourselves, enter into dialogue, and even into conflict, with others, which at the same time makes public the identity of our "opponent." In addition, we must demand just action on the part of the authorities who act as if justice in our country always keeps its eyes closed. For this initiative we need solidarity, a network of solidarity—things the widow and the woman suffering violence may well have experienced in the community of the saints. In short: Jesus counts on our faith, which proves itself active also in action on behalf of human and civil rights. Jesus counts on our participation.

2. Bound hands and feet, closed mouths, victims suffering violence, being too weak to resist: these are situationally-conditioned circumstances that Jesus also knows in our lives. Then he himself acts on our behalf. He is our counselor, he calls the authorities into question, he makes accusations and liberates from guilt. Jesus shows how we can encourage other people and help them to make a new beginning. Jesus counts on us to exercise our civil rights on behalf of others, that we be Christians for our neighbors. In the case of violence directed against women this means calling into question unjust patriarchal laws and

calling on Church and society to reflect on the consequences that such power has for the whole social fabric.

"Grant me justice against my opponent!" and "Let anyone among you who is without sin be the first to throw a stone at her!" represent two forms of the exercise of civil rights. Both are necessary. Both are political. Both are aware of the mechanisms of power in the law and government of the state. Both begin with the bodies and daily lives of women: violence and hope, love and pain, resistance and inconsolability, stubbornness and patience. And deeply rooted in all is tenderness, because we are convinced that we are already citizens of the royal reign of God. That enables us to look in the face of systems that reject and wound human rights and conquer them. Thus are stones made into bread.

Bibliography

Crüsemann, Frank. *Die Tora. Theologie und Sozialgeschichte des alttestamentlichen Gesetzes.* Munich: Kaiser, 1992. English: *The Torah: Theology and Social History of Old Testament Law.* Translated by Allan W. Mahnke. Minneapolis: Fortress, 1996.

Habermann, Ruth. "Das Evangelium nach Johannes. Orte der Frauen," in Luise Schottroff and Marie-Theres Wacker, eds., *Kompendium Feministische Bibelauslegung.* Gütersloh: Chr.Kaiser/Gütersloher Verlagshaus, 1998, 527–41.

Hauck, Friedrich. μοιχεύω, κτλ. *TDNT* 4:729–35.

Petermann (Batmartha), Ina Johanne. "Das Buch Ruth. Grenzgänge zweier Frauen im Patriarchat," in Luise Schottroff and Marie-Theres Wacker, eds., *Kompendium Feministische Bibelauslegung.* Gütersloh: Chr.Kaiser/Gütersloher Verlagshaus, 1998, 104–13.

Richter Reimer, Ivoni. "O poder dè uma protagonista. A oração de pessoas excluídas," *Revista de Interpretação Bíblica Latino-Americana (RIBLA)* 25 (1996) 63–73.

Schottroff, Luise. *Lydia's Impatient Sisters: A Feminist Social History of Early Christianity.* Translated by Barbara and Martin Rumscheidt. Louisville: Westminster John Knox, 1995, 101–18.

Choon-Ho You-Martin

"Women's Movements" and "Women's Theology." Social Change in South Korea between Tradition and Postmodernity

Christian women in South Korea are transgressive, walking the line between Eastern cultures and religions and Western Christianity, between tradition and the modern/postmodern, between the Third and the First World, between poverty and wealth, between war and peace, between militarism and democracy, and between patriarchy and women's liberation. They seek a Christian identity in the field of tension between Korean contextual specifics and universal problems. With courage and openness, therefore, they not infrequently cross their socially and individually fixed boundaries in order to free themselves from the complex of patriarchy and thereby to move from deadly structures into a *life with others*. A brief description of the women's movements and women's theology in South Korea will show how Christian women go to the limits of their swiftly changing life-context, and even dare to go beyond those limits when necessary. These women's courage in changing structures is at the heart of the forces of reform in church and society in South Korea on the threshold of the twenty-first century.

Women's Movements in the South Korean Context

Korean women in Confucian patrocentrism

Confucianism, or rather Neoconfucianism, which the Yi dynasty (1392–1910) made the basis of its national ideology, shapes Korean value systems and images of women in society as a whole at depth, even today. It is not a religion, but a kind of moral-philosophical doctrine from feudal times, based on a hierarchical-collective order of rank in five basic human relationships: ruler-subject, father-son, man-woman, older brother-younger brother, friend-friend. Ruler, father, man, and elder symbolize heaven, that is, absolute authority in each relationship. In this authoritarian system the father or husband is the center of family life in the sense of a strict patrocentrism. A woman, in contrast, is completely dependent throughout her life, first on her father, then on her husband, and later on her sons. The fundamental purpose of her existence is to be married and bear sons in order to secure the continuance of the family and tribe, and thus to sustain the patrilineal cult of the ancestors. Accordingly, the Confucian image of the ideal woman is that of "the wise mother (of sons) and good wife," expressed in absolute subjection and chastity (cf. Kim 1994, 203–15; Lee-Linke 1991, 18–71).

Even today the Confucian order of rank, gender, and age is perceptible in every aspect of life in Korea. Women in particular are required to practice the highest degree of feminine virtue, to sacrifice themselves for the good of the family. Social preference for sons and men above daughters and women is manifest in all social classes in the form of destruction of female fetuses through the instruments of modern medicine. The drastic consequences are becoming more and more evident in the uneven birth rate of daughters and sons (e.g., 100 to 115.4 in 1994; cf. *The Journal of Korean Feminist Theology* [1996] 97).

Women's movements and the ambivalent role of Christianity

Christianity's effect on Korean women's movements has been ambivalent. The modern, emancipatory women's movement in Korea began with the Protestant mission, which celebrated its centenary in 1984, proud of its "missionary miracle" (ca. 25% of the total population of South Korea calls itself Christian; 62% of these are women and 38% are men). The Christian teaching of the image of God in women and men was a truly liberating message for many women who lived under Confucian discrimination against women. Christianity awakened in women a new identity as human beings. In the early phases of the mission many newly-converted "churchwomen" or "Bible women" contributed to the explosive growth of the Church, even though they were often expelled from their traditional families because of their faith. They also fought on the socio-political level for women's education, for the reform of family law, and against wholesale prostitution. When Korea became a Japanese colony in 1910 the Christian Socialist women's movement spread through all classes in the wake of the independence movement.

This emancipatory women's movement quickly retreated as the Protestant churches were institutionalized and authoritarian-andro-centric Confucianism was "inculturated" into the hierarchical power system of Christianity. The twofold sexism in Confucianist-patriarchal Christianity intensified the oppression and marginalization of women enormously. Into the 1960s the activity of most Church women's groups was restricted to the caritative sphere and served the policies of the ruling elite. There was no mobilization of a broad basis of women in any form. Even now most Protestant denominations cling to their conservative-fundamentalist stance with regard to full participation of women in Church and society.

Women's movements as a response to the crisis of modernity

Korean women have found themselves since the beginning of the 1960s caught up in a rapid shift in values in which faith in unending growth and progress dominates the whole society as a quasi-religious grand ideology of modernity. South Korea rose within forty years from being a poor, agrarian society to a modern, urbanized industrial country (the eleventh-largest industrial nation in the world in 1996, according to the O.E.C.D.). Since the 1960s the country's economy has achieved a major expansion by means of an export-oriented economic policy and radical industrialization. The tempo of economic growth accelerated so rapidly until the mid-1990s that it constantly overtook political, social-ethical, and religious conceptualization (the annual rate of increase was as high as 12%: cf. Henseleit 1997, 94–116).

But the highly praised "economic miracle" in Korea left many destructive traces whose consequences were visible in urbanization, the exploitation of the work force, and environmental pollution. The quantitative economic growth demanded major sacrifices of the population and was sustained above all on the backs of women. Until the end of the 1970s the labor-intensive light industries (e.g., textiles, shoes, toys, pharmaceuticals, and electronics) produced the most important items of Korean export, and in most of those factories women constituted the majority of the labor force, working often under unacceptable conditions and earning scarcely half of what men received (41-54% on average) while working two or three hours longer each day than the men (cf. Kang and Lenz 1992, 39–45). In spite of the grandiose successes in the economy the profits benefited only a tiny proportion of the population, and most women lived in dire poverty. In the 1970s, out of necessity, a number of women's organizations, networks, and groups were formed. These women's groups "from below" fought against the minimal wages and poor working conditions of the factory workers, the increasing indebtedness of the farm women, and the extreme situation in the daily lives of the slum-dwellers (cf. Kang and Lenz 1992, 59–68). The women's groups from the middle and upper classes, on the other hand, concerned themselves primarily with socio-political topics such as democratization and the reunification of Korea.

Many women's groups, like other political opposition groups, were severely shaken after 1961 when three successive dictatorial military terror regimes transformed the country into a gigantic public prison. It was clear to them that the processes of democratization in the whole society and the practice of women's emancipation presupposed fundamental political change. In spite of the struggle of women throughout the country for liberation, the established women's groups from the middle and upper classes at first had scarcely any contact with the women in the basis movements. A separation within the women's movement occurred especially as a result of the militant activities of the worker women. With that, the problem of women's solidarity was concretely on the table, and the result was a confrontation with the class issue between women. A critical struggle with this problem was combined with controversial discussion of the relationship between sex, class, and capital interests.

Only at the beginning of the 1980s did a broad cooperation among women's groups from different classes come about as a result of the active engagement of the Christian women's associations (e.g., Korean Church Women United, the Korean Association of Women Theologians, and the Christian Women's Grassroots Organization) and the young academic women, who regarded the classes of the marginalized as having priority in the movement for women's liberation. Many groups of women made common cause for the abolition of the undemocratic constitution then in force, for actions in solidarity with women workers in industry, farm women, and slum-dwellers, for equal rights for women, for reunification, for social and economic justice, against the neocolonial powers in America and Japan, against Western cultural imperialism, and against the torture and rape of student women under arrest, etc. Thus the motives of the Christian and secular women's movements in the period between 1960 and 1987 were multidimensional, extending well beyond the Western gender-specific discussion of sexism.

Women's movements en route to civil society

After the social collapse of 1987/1988 there occurred a series of political and economic changes in South Korea: the process of democratization began and the military dictators were replaced by civil regimes.

The economic situation and working conditions have, for the most part, clearly improved. With the collapse of socialism and the impoverishment of North Korea (including both famine and a catastrophic economic situation) came a general restraint on the question of reunification. The country gradually began to display the typical features of a welfare, consumerist, leisure society. While in the struggle for liberation in the 1970s and 1980s "Minjung" (the marginalized, those suffering from oppression, exploitation, and alienation) was a code word for resistance, in the new social analyses the concept of "Simin" (citizen) was central. The "new" citizens understood themselves as a third power between state and economy. They took an interest in civic organizations not limited by class or party. Probably the most significant event in connection with the construction of civil networks was the foundation of the Korean Coalition of Citizens' Movements (KCCM), made up of thirty-six different civic organizations, in September 1994 (cf. Wein 1997, 41–66).

A large number of women's organizations joined the new citizens' movements. They participated both in the stabilization of civil society and in the expansion of regional and global cooperation in various fields. The principal aims of the women's movement since the end of the 1980s have been: equal rights for women, child care, the elimination of violence against women, environmental protection, sustainable ecology, disarmament and peace in northern Asia, the reunification of Korea, an alternative economic order, consumer protection, etc. Some key proposals of intensive women's campaigns were made reality through constitutional change: an equal rights law for men and women (1988), reform of the labor laws for improvement/equality of working women (1989), reform of family law in favor of wives, divorced women, widows, and daughters (1991), and protection of women against violence in their families (1998).

Somewhat later than the transformation of society, the democratization of the churches was also set in motion. Countless church basis groups of women, ecumenical coordinating organizations, and women theologians advocated over decades for equality of the sexes in the churches. Within and outside the institutional Church, the "church women" created a variety of organizations and initiatives, carried out consciousness-raising projects, struggled against discrimination against women in congregations, and hand in hand with academic women developed a Korean women's theology. One visible fruit of the women's movement in the churches was the authorization of women's ordination in the PCK (Presbyterian Church of Korea), one of the largest denominations in South Korea, in 1994. On the occasion of the ecumenical Women's Decade and the challenge to a "theology of life," Christian women now sought to construct new forms of community of faith and life (e.g., creation of the Women's Church, cooperative dwelling arrangements for single women on an ecological farm, and old-age assistance for church women).

Challenges of globalization to the women's movements

Since the most recent economic crisis in Asia in 1997/1998 women in South Korea have been confronted daily with the essence of economic globalization, and that in the drastic form of international financial speculation, forced reforms through the structural accommodation policies of the IMF, devaluation of currency, debt crises, bankruptcy of firms and factories, inflation, and mass unemployment. Within six months after the "big bang" in November 1997 the total unemployment rose to two million (a rise in the unemployment rate from 3% to 5%, which in the Korean context is relatively high), and inflation rose to 8.2%, while the rate of economic growth sank rapidly (–3.8%). The new civil regime, which was placed under IMF trusteeship, was unable to function politically or economically. In particular, the new poverty once again showed a female face: preference for early dismissal of women workers and employees without any kind of social insurance, budgetary strangulation through mass unemployment, inflation, and increase of violence against women occasioned by social unrest are among the clear signs (cf. Mayer 1997, 1–3; *The Kidok Kong Bo in Korea* [20 June 1998] 3).

Christian and secular women's groups reacted quickly to the threat of national collapse. They produced emergency aid for the unemployed, the homeless, children, women, and old people, for families affected by the "IMF cold wave" who received no aid from the state. To ease the national debt crisis (more than U.S. $200 billion) women throughout the land began campaigns for contributions of gold and against the importation of luxury goods. They organized "green exchange ring initiatives" everywhere. However, these actions were short-term tiny drops on a hot stone. Increasingly, women discovered that the Korean people would no longer be able to compete and survive in the twenty-first century without structural change in the socioeconomic, political, and ecological realms. In face of the challenges of the world economic order they are now seeking alternative ways of life in the period of globalization, sustainability of the economy, and retraining of the female work force. The Christian women's movement has, in addition to these pragmatic initiatives, the important task of showing the women thus affected new ways to a lifegiving spirituality.

Feminist-Liberation-Oriented Women's Theology in South Korea

Origins of Korean women's theology in the
context of the Minjung movement

The development of a feminist-liberation-oriented consciousness among Korean women theologians began around the middle of the 1970s in connection with the political Minjung-liberation movement. The Sino-Korean concept of the "Minjung" (literally "mass of the people") describes the groups of people who are "politically oppressed, economically exploited, socially alienated, and from the cultural and intellectual point of view kept in a situation of ignorance" (Hyen 1985, 4). To these groups belonged for the most part workers, farmers, slum-dwellers, labor unionists, students and intellectuals who fought against the military dictatorship and the neo-capitalistic economic power in the country. They advocated primarily for democracy, respect for human rights, economic and social justice, national self-determination, and the reunification of Korea. The political process of consciousness-building was accompanied by a renaissance of Korean culture (Minjung culture) and religious reform movements. Constitutive for the conscious identity of the Minjung movement was a new interpretation of Korean history as a history of suffering by the simple people who were at the same time to be regarded as the subjects of their own history. Among the representatives of this opposition movement Christians were in the minority, but they quickly formulated their own experiences of suffering into an inductive, political theology of liberation in the Korean context (Minjung theology), and later established Minjung communities. They sought to free the oppressed from their suffering through a comprehensive change in society (cf. Küster 1995, 105–78).

Quite a few women theologians and churchwomen participated in this Minjung movement, but soon after beginning this common resistance work they perceived that gender-specific oppression of women was not taken seriously by the male Minjung theologians. The manifold forms of discrimination against women in patriarchal structures, combined with the modernized socio-economic, political, and religious-cultural situation of the country (women as "Minjung among the Minjung"), were not a subject of interest for the liberation theologians. Thus the Minjung women began to express, from the perspective of Korean women, their struggle for life, survival, and liberation from the manifold forms of oppression. As early as 1980 Korean women theologians joined in the Korean Association of Women Theologians (KAWT) to advance the establishment of feminist liberation theology in the Korean context. From the beginning they demanded their right to autonomy in doing theology: that is, their independence from having their thinking prescribed either by androcentric Third World male liberation theologies or by eurocentric Western feminist theologies. In doing so they were in accord with the chief aim of the women's commissions in the CCA (Christian Conference of Asia, whose women's division was created in 1981) and EATWOT (Ecumenical Association of Third World Theologians, women's division created 1983: cf. Fabella 1996, 58–76). They no longer regarded sexism as the sole analytical category for feminist theology, but developed a contextual critique of patriarchy capable of comprehending the interweaving and mutual influence of various forms of women's oppression *qua* gender, race, class, religion, economics, political and cultural adherence, etc. in the Korean context.

Like many feminists in the Third world, these women criticized the hidden eurocentrism, universalism, racism, cultural imperialism, neo-colonialism, and neo-capitalism of Western feminism and its restriction to the struggle against sexism. In the second and third generations of women's theology the perception of cultural differences between patriarchy in Korea and in the Western world has steadily increased (cf. Chung 1990). A universal critique of sexism has been replaced by a search for a pluralistic feminism and an appreciation for women's contextually different strategies for liberation. In agreement with other Asiatic women liberation theologians, the Korean women describe their theology as "women's theology." The preference for "women's theology" instead of "feminist theology" has a tactical basis, since the concept of feminism, which is viewed as a kind of Western decadence, is broadly rejected in this society.

Sources and tasks of women's theology

A principal source of Korean women's theology is the specific experience of women's suffering in the Korean context. Some Minjung women theologians, together with male Minjung theologians, have found an expression for the experience of suffering by the oppressed. They call this collectively and individually experienced injustice caused by structural sin "Han." Most women experience "Han within Han," because their experiences of oppression are more complex and painful than those of men in the Korean context. The goal of women's theology is the liberation of the suffering from their "Han," accomplished in the midst of the liberating actions of God in history. The process of liberation from "Han"—corresponding to the process of healing in Korean shamanism—is called "Han-pu-ri" (cf. Chung 1989, 135–46; 1990). In the liberation process women are the subjects of their own socio-biography and thus are also the "text" of feminist liberation theology. For many Korean women, who live in a culture of death and silence, it is enormously important to discover their identity and their existence as subjects in the reality of their own lives. Another source of this theology is a critical awareness that is capable of uncovering the ideology of subjection. A third source is constituted by the cultural and religious traditions of Korea, the oppressive aspects of which are critically investigated while the liberating traditions are appropriated. A fourth source is the Bible. There is a vivid and controversial discussion in progress over the authority of the Bible, the Christian claim to absolutism, christological dogmas, and the institutional Church as criteria or hermeneutical keys for women's theology. In this process it has become more and more clear to Korean women that the significance of the Bible is not to be measured by its agreement with Church tradition, but by whether the Bible empowers the people plagued by Han to recover their full humanity and free themselves so that they have the strength to live.

The task of women's theology is, accordingly, the comprehensive liberation of women, men, society, and nature from the complex structural sins of patriarchy. Korean women theologians often emphasize that men are also included in their struggle for liberation, because their aim is liberation of both women and men in a transformed world. "Liberation" in the Korean context means a wholistic healing of the human, the society, and the cosmos. Necessarily, in the process of healing and salvation the displacement of Western anthropocentrism becomes an Asiatic life-centering in which people understand themselves anew as a part of creation and respect the earth as the mother of all life (cf. Chung 1990; Küster 1995, 158–72; Strahm 1997, 60–85).

Methods in women's theology

The theologial methods of women's theology as developed by the KAWT resemble Korean shamanistic ritual ("Kut"), for in the center of Korean women's theology as well as in Korean shamanism is the overcoming of suffering ("Han-pu-ri"). Shamans help people through various rituals, sacrificial offerings, dances, and songs to free themselves from their Han-plagued lives or at least to lighten their suffering. Analogously to the role of the shaman, the women theologians should act as "priests of Han" and deliver oppressed women from suffering to new life. The methods of Korean women's theology are, like those of most liberation theologies, inductive; they are collective and ecumenical in their procedures, inclusive in their goals, and proceed in four circular steps (cf. Lee-Park 1985, 172–82; Fabella 1996, 150–51; Chung 1990; Strahm 1997, 75–85).

1. Women's Storytelling and Active Listening: The women theologians listen to the socio-biographies of individual women (for the concept of socio-biography see Kim 1984/85, 66–78). The power of oral narrative of one's own life brings the hidden social complexities of the truth of women's lives into the awareness of both the teller and the listeners.

2. Critical Analysis of Patriarchy: Patriarchy is here recognized as an all-inclusive structural system pervading the entire social structure, laws, norms, customs, and personal and collective ways of behaving. Korean women therefore base their theology not simply on a gender-specific analysis of sexism, but on a comprehensive (sociological, economic, political, ecological, religious, cultural, and psychological) analysis of patriarchy and the connections among various mechanisms of oppression. Among the often-discussed structural sins of patriarchy in the Korean context are Confucianism, collectivism, militarism, neo-capitalism, cultural imperialism, neo-colonialism, racism, and sexism.

3. Theological Reflection: The Bible serves as a source of wisdom about life, but not as the absolute and unchangeable truth from God. For too long a time the authority of the Bible was misused to maintain Western cultural imperialism in Korea and to devalue indigenous religious and cultural traditions as superstition. Together with interpretation of the Bible from the perspective of Korean women, the culture and religions of the country (Buddhism, Taoism, Confucianism, shamanism, and animism) furnish important sources for theological reflection. Women delve after their own roots, in myths, legends, songs, poems, dances, painting, and women's spirituality. However, all these sources are read anew from the perspective of women and tested to see whether they advance the dignity and self-determination of women or legitimate their oppression.

4. Actions to Overcome Unjust Situations, Here and Now: Korean women call this way of doing theology in the concrete praxis of life "Hyun-jang theology." ("Hyun-jang" translates as the present place in which historical events are occurring.) Women theologians are working on a theology that stands in direct relationship with the daily struggle of women for life. Thus they are engaged, for example, in combating sex tourism and the trade in women, the killing of female fetuses, and the torture of imprisoned women students, and in favor of child care centers in the poor districts of the cities. In solidarity with other women the Hyun-jang theologians are learning how high the costs of a lived women's theology can be.

New tasks for Korean women's theology in the
paradigm shift from modernity to postmodernity

The themes and concepts of women's theology in Korea are varied, controversial, contextual, and global, for they reflect the open, dynamic processes by which Korean women are discovering their identity within the rapid social change that is occurring as part of an epochal paradigm shift from modernity to postmodernity. Since the 1970s the highest values of modernity, such as growth, progress, rationality, efficiency, uniformity, universality, and dominance have been represented everywhere in the society as the driving forces of the country's modernization. Patriarchal mechanisms of oppression were modified in accord with this *Zeitgeist* of modernity, closely linked with globalization in market economics and with the way of life associated with an industrial work-and-production society.

On the other hand, it cannot be overlooked that the growing self-awareness of the Korean people demanded a discovery of both collective and individual identity in their own life-context. In contrast to the economic globalization and uniform internationalism of modernity, to a growing extent the rediscovery of their own culture and history has become the critical locus for the people's construction of its own identity. The Minjung women theologians in particular rejected the universal-historical concepts of Western theologies and the *ratio,* the god of modernity, as a universally valid criterion for judging Christian action. Women's theologies in Korea were accordingly created not on the basis of rational doctrines, but out of the concrete life experiences of women in the Korean context, the search for wholistic life-events, and pluralistic and contextualized apprehensions of truth. The comprehensive system of theology that incorporates the whole world was abandoned in favor of the locally relevant systems of women. Some important concepts in Korean women's theology, such as contextuality, pluralism, experiences, event, life-centering, wholistic spirituality, and post-patriarchal overcoming of dualism between men and women, however, are precisely the fundamental categories of postmodernity (for the modernity-postmodernity discussion see Sundermeier 1994, 293–310; Küng 1988; 1991).

A good many Korean women theologians are thoroughly aware that they stand in the midst of the transition process from modernity to postmodernity. They are posing new questions in light of this epochal transformation: What effect will this paradigm shift have on the elementary human search for security and meaning? Will Christian women be in a position to reappropriate the challenges of postmodernity in the biblical witness and to give new validity to respect for the rights proper to all parts of God's creation? What is a good, successful life in the post-modern age? Feminist discussion in Korea in recent years has intensified the demands for rethinking androcentrism and anthropocentrism, the characteristic thought models of modernity, in favor of life-centeredness, concentrating it on the concepts of *diakonia*, solidarity, and women's spirituality.

If women wish to embody a new Church that seeks a sustainable community of life on earth it is necessary that, besides their diaconal activities at the local level, they at the same time seek to exercise solidarity with women throughout the world. For local problems are no longer solely based on contextual specifics; instead, they interact with global causes and consequences. A further central task of Korean women's theology in the future is the development of a wholistic women's spirituality. Many signs indicate that the challenges post-modernity poses for the Church will concentrate especially in this area. Wholistic women's spirituality is thus not a mystical, world-denying spirituality of withdrawal from the world, the ascesis and spiritual exercises of one set apart. Instead, it is a spirituality "lived" every day on behalf of life, working as a liberating, woman-affirming, nature-protecting, and creation-centered power. Its goal is the wholistic salvation of women, men, and God's whole created universe.

Challenges of tomorrow's world

Not only Korean women, but we, all the women of the world, stand before the enormous challenges of socio-economic, political, religio-cultural, technical, and ecological globalization. An epochal paradigm shift from modernity to postmodernity is already in process. In light of this Janus face of our age we, as post-patriarchal transgressive women, need actions of solidarity between East-West women and South-North women more than ever. Neoliberal globalization in the market economy, the gap between rich and poor, the ecological imperilment of the earth, conflicts in cultures and religions, and the unreconciled society of women and men are both worldwide and regional problems. Only together can we gather the strength to contribute to the development of viable and sustainable forms of human community that are in harmony with the right to life of the whole creation. Decisive, as we proceed on our way to the world of tomorrow, will be the extent to which the women of the world dare to open themselves for and with one another and in solidarity to take courageous steps across the boundaries of contemporary history. Will we women in all continents, despite all the insecurities and risks involved, walk together on the road into the twenty-first century?

Bibliography

Asian Women Doing Theology. Report from the Singapore Conference, November 20–29, 1987. Hong Kong: Asian Women's Resource Center for Culture and Theology, 1989.

Chung, Hyun-Kyung. *Struggle to Be the Sun Again: Introducing Asian Women's Theology.* Maryknoll, N.Y.: Orbis, 1990.

_____. "'Han-pu-ri': Doing Theology from Korean Women's Perspective," in Virginia Fabella and Sun Ai Lee-Park, eds., *We Dare to Dream. Doing Theology as Asian Women.* Hong Kong: Asian Women's Resource Center for Culture and Theology, 1989, 135–46.

Drescher, Lutz. "Ende des Wachstums? Die protestantischen Kirchen Südkoreas in der Krise," *ZfM* 20 (1995) 105–16.

Fabella, Virginia. "Der Weg der Frauen. Theologinnen der Dritten Welt melden sich zu Wort," in *Theologie der Dritten Welt* 22. Freiburg, Basel, and Vienna: Herder, 1996.

Henseleit, Rainer. "Südkorea: Wirtschaftstrends zur Jahresmitte 1997," in Patrick Köllner, ed., *Korea 1997. Politik, Wirtschaft, Gesellschaft.* Hamburg: Institut für Asienkunde, 1997, 94–116.

Hyun, Young-Hak. "Minjung: The Suffering Servant and Hope," *Inter-Religio* 7 (1985) 2–14.

Kang, Chong-Sook, and Ilse Lenz. *Wenn die Hennen krähen—: Frauenbewegung in Korea.* Münster: Westfälisches Dampfboot, 1992.

Kim, Victoria Jung-Hi. "Das konfuzianische Bild der Frau in der koreanischen Choson-Dynastie (1392–1910)," *ZMR* 78/3 (1994) 203–15.

Kim, Yong-Bok. "Theology and the Social-Biography of Minjung," *CTC Bulletin* 5/3; 6/1 (1984–1985) 66–78.

Küng, Hans. *Global Responsibility: In Search of a New World Ethic.* Translated by John Bowden. New York: Crossroad, 1991.

_____. *Theology for the Third Millennium: An Ecumenical View.* Translated by Peter Heinegg. New York: Doubleday, 1988.

Küster, Volker. *Theologie im Kontext. Zugleich ein Versuch über die Minjung-Theologie.* Nettetal: Steyler, 1995.

Lee-Linke, Sung-Hee. *Frauen gegen Konfuzius. Perspektiven einer asiastisch-feministischen Theologie.* Gütersloh: Gerd Mohn, 1991.

Lee-Park, Sun Ai. "Asian Women's Theological Reflection," *East Asia Journal of Theology* 3/2 (1985) 172–82.

Mayer, Peter. "Südkorea in der Wirtschaftskrise. Zur Situation am Ende des Jahres 1997," *Koreaforum* 7/2 (1997) 1–3.

Park, Jong-Chun. "A Paradigm Change in Korean Indigenization Theology: From Theology of 'Sincerity' to Interliving Theology," in Joon-Surh. Park and Naozumi Eto, *Theology and Theological Education in Asia: Today and Tomorrow: the 25th anniversary theological symposium of NEAATS, June 18–20, 1992, Kansai Seminar House, Kyoto, Japan.* Seoul: North East Asia Association of Theological Schools, 1992, 19–109.

"Spirituality for Life: Women Struggling Against Violence," *Voices from the Third World* 12 (1994) 1.

Sundermeier, Theo. "Pluralismus, Fundamentalismus, Koinonia," *Evangelische Theologie* 54/4 (1994) 293–310.

Strahm, Doris. *Vom Rand in die Mitte. Christologie aus der Sicht von Frauen in Asien, Afrika und Lateinamerika.* Theologie in Geschichte und Gesellschaft 4. Luzern: Exodus, 1997.

The Journal of Korean Feminist Theology 28 (1996).

Wein, Roland. "Südkorea auf dem Weg zur Zivilgesellschaft: Die Zivilgesellschaftsorganisationen," in Patrick Köllner, ed., *Korea 1997. Politik, Wirtschaft, Gesellschaft.* Hamburg: Institut für Asienkunde, 1997, 41–66.

Eske Wollrad

On Getting Out of One's Skin:
Depictions of White Femininity in Film

As long as you think you're white,
there's no hope for you.

—James Baldwin, as quoted by David Roediger

Once upon a time there was an emperor. Two tailors came to him and told him they could make clothes for him that were only visible to the wise, but could not be seen by fools. The emperor was charmed and asked them to make the clothes. Everyone admired them—the emperor, his ministers, all the people—so as not to appear fools, although no one could see them. But finally, when the naked emperor paraded through the cheering crowds, a child revealed the lie by crying out: "But he hasn't got any clothes on!"

Whiteness is one of the most efficient lies produced by modernity. Equipped with the qualities of intellectual and moral superiority, beauty, reason, and purity, whiteness was attributed to certain bodies that had no similarity to each other, either genetic or phenotypic. Since the seventeenth century whiteness has been attributed to or imposed on people; it could be purchased or seized by force, but at no point was it unmistakable and visible. Whiteness is, rather, a political category that is supposed to explain why certain people have privileges and others do not. The African-American writer James Baldwin described the fictional character of whiteness and could only shake his head over those who, in their self-fascination, admired themselves for something (a supposedly "natural" superiority) that simply does not exist.

In order that people will believe the fiction of whiteness to be true, an ideological machinery is brought into play to present whiteness as the signature of everything good, everything divine, for progress, reason, civilization, and order. To this machinery belongs what is called "popular

111

culture." Here I am especially interested in one sector of popular culture, namely film. Contemporary theologians continue to nurse a deep mistrust of this genre, perhaps because they know that "images are existentially more powerful than texts" (Flusser 1997, 138) and that film, as a sense-oriented spectacle, is more capable than words of drawing people under its spell. When films are theologically analyzed at all, it is only the so-called "good" or "cultured" films, never Hollywood's mass production numbers—which is astonishing when one considers that Hollywood films treat, in impressive fashion, such themes as guilt and forgiveness ("Dead Man Walking"), purgatory and life after death ("Star Trek: The Next Generation"), and the relationship between science and faith ("Contact"). These films illustrate answers to theological questions in a monumental style that permits no distancing. "Hollywood has developed an aesthetics of narrative cinema that excludes any form of distanced view" (Schlüpmann 1994, 83).

The aesthetics of White[1] femininity presented by Hollywood are as fascinating as they are multilayered. The British scholar Richard Dyer studies both films for the big screen and TV movies; he finds that White women's role is usually to stand helplessly by and say: "There's nothing I can do!" (Dyer 1997, 187). Hollywood productions in which strong men are chosen to save the world or the whole universe show White women as those who wait anxiously until, after the battle is won, they can fold their tousled heroes in their arms ("Independence Day," "Armageddon"). But there are other films in which White femininity stands for power and dominance, films that illustrate the aesthetics of White feminine exercise of power with the aid of religious symbolism. I will use the film "Dangerous Minds" to show the basic patterns according to which Whiteness, gender, class, and Christianity are combined and presented.

"Dangerous Minds," appearing in 1995, is about a special kind of trespass. The film places its White protagonist not in the macro-realm of the world drama, but in the micro-realm of a California school. It is about a White woman named LouAnne Johnson (played by Michelle Pfeiffer), who after her divorce from her violent husband and after nine years of military service decides to become an English teacher. And although she is only a student teacher, she immediately gets a full-time job in a northern California high school. There is a catch, however: the class she is supposed to teach is "special," because it is made up of undisciplined African-American and Latin-American students.

---

[1] The capitalization of "White" and "Black" is meant to make clear that these concepts (when applied to human beings) are not biological, but socially constructed categories, invented to validate certain power relationships.

LouAnne's first day at school ends in a fiasco: she is taunted and humiliated by the class.

Her White friend and mentor Hal consoles her, and LouAnne decides to try a different tack: the next day she shows up "tough," in jeans and a leather jacket, tells the students she is an ex-soldier, and demonstrates some karate moves. That impresses the class, but not the African-American principal, Mr. Grandy, who forbids her ever again to use such unconventional teaching methods. But LouAnne doesn't let herself be beaten: by means of all sorts of tricks and turns she succeeds in awakening an interest in learning in most of the students. Still, LouAnne also suffers some defeats: two of the Black students, Kareem and Big G, leave school because they have to earn money. Then there is also the uppity Emilio, a drug dealer who is always disturbing the class. When he receives a death threat from one of his competitors, LouAnne tries to help him, but unsuccessfully: Emilio is shot to death. Callie also leaves because she is pregnant and the principal tells her she should transfer to a school for housekeeping.

LouAnne decides to quit. We never learn why. Because of Emilio's death? Or because Kareem, Big G, and Callie have left school? But on the last day of school she changes her mind: Callie is back and has decided to finish school, and the students beg LouAnne to stay: "You are our light!"

The Subject Is White

One pattern followed also by "Dangerous Minds" is the pretense that the film is about so-called minorities and their problems (thus also "Mississippi Burning" and "Amistad"). According to Dyer, the White protagonists are constantly concerned for the "minorities," but the films never show us their point of view (cf. Dyer 1997, 196). The very positioning of the cameras shows who is really central, who has feelings and a story. For "positioning is positioning" (Gertrud Koch 1992). The camera only follows LouAnne: from the school to her house, into her living room, into her bedroom, into a café. We see only that part of the students' lives and world that LouAnne sees. "The film tells us nothing about the lives of the students themselves. The audience is given no notion of their stories and experiences outside of school" (Giroux 1997, 299). Only LouAnne's story counts, and she has abundant opportunity to tell the audience about her past, her feelings, and her experiences. The loving eye of the camera leaves us in no doubt about whose ego is exclusively at issue. "In this film the children appear only as a background for the expansion of LouAnne's self-confidence and self-image, rather than offering us an opportunity to understand their growing up or how racism functions in the school and in society as a whole" (Giroux 1997, 300).

The Color of Money

At the very beginning of the film we learn that LouAnne receives $2058 per month in this job. In spite of that she can afford countless chocolate bars as rewards for correct answers, a trip to the amusement park for the whole class, and a dinner for four in a fine restaurant, and can lend her student Raul $200. Where does she get the money? If LouAnne were a Black woman the film would have had to explain at length what her financial resources are and make it clear that she obtained the money honorably. If LouAnne were a White woman without means the film would have explained just as clearly how and why she had gotten into such a regrettable situation. Only what is "normal" needs no explanation, and in Hollywood the normal color of money is White.

LouAnne's comfortable status is presented in the film as something just as natural as the poverty of the Black and Hispanic students. For LouAnne it is nothing special that her Black student Callie has to work in the supermarket every day after school. When the Black students Kareem and Big G leave school LouAnne attempts to explain to their grandmother how important an education is. She, however, answers sharply: "Bills have to be paid. If you want to play the savior you'll have to get some other boys." The grandmother hits the nail on the head: LouAnne wants to be a savior, but she is not the least bit interested in the living conditions of her "proteges."

Trespassing: White Civilization in the Jungle

The opening credits of the film leave no doubt about the milieu with which LouAnne will have to contend: in grainy black and white photography we see homeless people searching dumpsters, watch dealers selling drugs, and hear police sirens. The soundtrack rap bears the revealing title "Gangsta's Paradise." The film peddles the stereotypes that reduce Black and Hispanic neighborhoods to poverty, drugs, and crime. Hence it is not surprising to see the children of that neighborhood climb over tables and benches in school. When LouAnne comes jauntily into the class on her first day she recoils because the students are chattering, drumming (!) and dancing to ear-splitting rap music. The setting evokes imaginary phantoms of the fearful jungle with its uncontrollable wild creatures.

The depiction of the confrontation between White civilization and Black wildness is nothing new; it is the basic pattern of many a Hollywood film, from Westerns through safari movies to science fiction. In "Dangerous Minds," however, the unique and tension-filled factor is that here it is not the muscular White hero who confronts the "wild things," but a White woman in a lacy blouse. "Because she leaves the security of her white middle-class culture to teach in a cultural war zone filled with chaos and potential danger, LouAnne Johnson is presented to the audience as an innocent trespasser. This image of innocence and good will offers White America the comforting belief that disorder, ignorance, and chaos are always somewhere else—in this strange, homogeneous, racial space known as the big-city ghetto" (Giroux 1997, 298). How will this innocent, tender creature—the very model of White femininity—conquer the dark chaos?

White Lies, White Ethics

In "Dangerous Minds" the ethics of the white lie, bribery, and tricks are presented as appropriate means for the upbringing of Black and Hispanic students. LouAnne doesn't teach, she trains. In one scene we see how she applies what she calls her "secret weapon": LouAnne tosses a chocolate bar to every student who answers a question correctly, just as in the circus a trick well performed merits a reward. To motivate her students to interpret a poem, LouAnne promises them a trip to an amusement park. Of course the class is suspicious and asks who will pay for it. LouAnne answers jauntily: "the school board." That is a flat lie. When the Black principal later confronts her about the trip, LouAnne says that the students begged her to come with them and she was so moved that she paid for all of them. When the principal warns her that it is not permissible to pay for the interpretation of a poem that way, LouAnne says sharply: "In my class poetry is its own reward." The audience knows that is a lie.

Finally, she announces a contest: whoever finds a certain poem will win a dinner at the best restaurant in town. But the contest is scarcely over before LouAnne announces to the baffled class that learning itself is the prize. The ability to think, she says, is an important weapon, and "I want to arm you for this dangerous world." That is quite a noble claim, especially when one considers that she was the one who had presented material reward as the prize for a scholarly achievement. The producers of the film, Don Simpson and Jerry Bruckheimer, consider the ethics of lying, bribery, and competition for material advantages to be a model: "We wanted to show her [LouAnne's] struggle with the system, with the kids, and with the environment in which the kids are growing up . . . and to demonstrate that these teachers really are important models" (from an interview on movieweb.com).

The Weapons of White Pedagogy

What materials does LouAnne Johnson choose with which to arm her students for the dangerous world? With amazing self-confidence (after all, she is only a student teacher and has no experience at all in teaching) LouAnne immediately tosses out the existing lesson plans and becomes creative: for grammar practice she uses the sentence "I want to die," and later she has the students interpret the text of Bob Dylan's "Mr. Tambourine Man," about dealers and addicts. The object of the contest then is to find a poem by the White British poet Dylan Thomas (1914–1953) that resembles the text of the song. LouAnne has no doubt that death, drugs, and violence are the prime topics for these youths, and that it is appropriate to discuss a song from LouAnne's own youth, that is, one that was written almost twenty years earlier, before the students were born. The film conveys that only sources from White culture—classic or popular—are appropriate teaching material. The students represent the precivilized and therefore prehistoric, history-less, and cultureless stage; they have no culture that belongs in the lessons.

Worse still: they are not even permitted to determine their own story. "Dangerous Minds" is based on an autobiographical book by the ex-soldier and teacher LouAnne Johnson. In the press release she says: "First I thought it was a little presumptuous to write about teaching when I had only been doing it for three years. But then I saw that it was not my story; it was the story of my kids, and I knew that if I could bring them onto paper it could help other kids who are confronted by similar obstacles" (movieweb.com). Johnson writes about "her" kids; she is—even after only three years of teaching—their only voice. Prehistoric primitiveness is speechless, and with it Hispanic and African-American history and culture. The film imagines White culture not as the best and most valuable, but as the only one in existence.

The White Power of Definition

LouAnne embodies faith in the illusion that all people can do whatever they want if they only try hard and are diligent. It is the American Dream: anyone can who wants to. LouAnne promotes an ethic that postulates that all people, seen as individuals, and their achievements can be judged in terms of individual effort. She says: "There are no victims in this class." With this definition she denies the existence of power structures that make Blacks and Latinos/Latinas victims and from which women like LouAnne profit. Second, LouAnne presumes that all people have access to a spectrum of possible ways of acting from which they can choose their options in any given situation. In her second day in class she asserts: "you always have a choice." This postulate permits her and the audience to ignore the fact that having a variety of choices is the privilege of a few. The womanist theologian Katie Cannon writes: "The Black woman in particular is often required to carefully consider a will that is not her own" (Cannon 1988, 144).

The Dark Peril

In classic Africa movies and science fiction films it is the White hero who, as the embodiment of civilization, penetrates the unknown wilderness and masters every attacker. In "Dangerous Minds," too, the hero LouAnne has to fight against opposing forces that stand in the way of her goal, bringing knowledge to the students. But it is not racist persons and/or institutions that make LouAnne's life difficult. It is the Blacks themselves. The principal, Mr. Grandy, embodies the pedantic pen-pusher who is only concerned with forms and appears to have no interest in the intellectual development of his students. Since he refuses to listen to LouAnne's student Emilio when he is in mortal danger, he is indirectly responsible for Emilio's murder. He is also the one who advises Callie to leave school because she is pregnant. Finally, the Black grandmother is solely responsible for the fact that Kareem and Big G stay away from class. She and Grandy represent, on the one hand, the dark peril that threatens to overturn the civilizing project, and on the other hand the "dumb Blacks" who do not know what is good for them. In this way the film reproduces the racist supposition that "white teachers alone are able to bring order, decency, and hope to those on the margins of society" (Giroux 1997, 304).

"I Am the Light of the World."
Christian Symbolism and Female Mission

The theologian Arno Schilson is right: "Religion awakens, not in the churches, but in the midst of the secular, to an unsuspected new life" (Schilson 1997, 28). The new life constitutes itself through the indissoluble connection that the religious forges with the imaginary-symbolic world of the film. While Christian film research has thus far concentrated overwhelmingly on investigating films in which Christian themes are explicitly addressed (as in Scorsese's "The Last Temptation of Christ"), "Dangerous Minds" shows how Christian symbolism creates deeper complexes of meaning and produces explanations without which the dominance of White femininity would lose its legitimacy.

The symbolism of light runs throughout the film, both verbally and visually. The students are to interpret a poem by Dylan Thomas about "raging against the dying of the light." Darkness as a threatening danger is taken up again near the end of the film when LouAnne decides to leave the school. It is the students themselves who call LouAnne their light, whose extinguishing would mean the end of these young people's hope and future. The references to the Johannine "I am" sayings remain subtle because the film is intended for Western Christian cultural circles and presumes that the audience is familiar with Christian metaphors of light. In addition, the film works with the Christian connection between the light theme and that of salvation/ redemption: LouAnne quite explicitly claims the function of the savior when she says to Raul, "I am your only way out." Similarly, she says to Emilio: "If you take my advice it will give your whole life a new direction."

The film builds the Johannine light-darkness dualism into a concept of "race"; that is, it orders light and darkness to Black and White individuals and hierarchizes the relationship. In this way White predominance, embodied in the White savior, achieves its metaphysical legitimation. But the dualism cannot remain static, because the essence of Christianity is expansion: all those who walk in darkness must be brought to the light, for the Christian mission accepts no limitations. In "Dangerous Minds" expansion as civilizing mission is illustrated, although the film carefully distinguishes between those who can be saved (Raul, Callie, etc.) and those who are lost forever (Kareem and Big G's grandmother, Mr. Grandy). That is the credo of American dominance: there is no ultimate Other, for even the primitive and dark can be led to the light. "The primitive always already contains the seed of civilization as potential for overcoming itself with the aid of civilizing assistance" (Langford 1998, 254). LouAnne offers her students nothing less than the opportunity to become White by assenting to a capitalist consumer orientation and internalizing White values. That this is not only possible for Black and Hispanic students, but is already happening, is expressed in the film not verbally, but visually: in the course of the action the young people's clothes become lighter and lighter, an effect of which the wardrobe designer, Bobbie Read, is especially proud (movieweb.com).

The White Transgressor Woman

The film first overcomes sex-specific limitations: it does not operate within the boundaries of traditional gender roles, which reserve penetration of the wilderness for White men. "Dangerous Minds" refutes the idea that action, discovery, taming, and conquering are White male virtues (so Dyer 1994, 73). LouAnne acts here, and not as an assistant in the wake of a male hero, but quite independently, though of course within the traditionally female realm of secondary education. This aspect functions to indicate to White middle-class women what their place is, because it describes the sphere within which they can and should exercise power.

The problem with the film is that it depicts a crossing of boundaries that aims at the removal of boundaries (LouAnne brings light into the darkest corner), and at the same time it needs those boundaries in order to legitimate LouAnne's claim to the space beyond the border. For she is White and is superior only in contrast to her Black subordinates. "Only the presence of Blacks permits . . . Whiteness to be seen as Whiteness and allows for the construction of a 'white femininity'" (Lippert 1994, 97). The White femininity that LouAnne represents combines traditional male characteristics like reason, civilization, order, and control with the attributes of innocence and purity that are so important precisely because White femininity is always in danger of "slipping down" into the darkness, because it is always thought of in connection with sexuality, the female "defilement" per se. LouAnne is present as asexual and therefore as White, innocent, and pure. The concomitant to this ideal White femininity, however, is anything but positive: while the Black and Hispanic students dance, scream, beat each other, and die, LouAnne remains strangely unembodied and lifeless. She is never wounded in body or in soul; she never loses her control, and even in her sorrow over Emilio's death she remains entirely the Lady.

White femininity is a deeply relational category and a construction that must constantly reassert itself in its difference from the imaginary Other. Hollywood presents White female trespass as penetration of the other, the dark, and depicts "racial" war zones that on the one hand signal chaos and danger and on the other hand open space for active participation in the terror of White domination. "Dangerous Minds" celebrates the real danger: the White disembodied and lifeless missionary with an unbounded claim to power.

The trespasser is the terrorist.

The End[2]

[2] I am grateful to Silke Hinder and Rita Wawrzinek for their constructive criticism.

Bibliography

Bollmann, Stefan, ed. *Medienkultur Vilém Flusser.* Frankfurt am Main: Fischer Taschenbuch, 1997.

Cannon, Katie G. *Black Womanist Ethics.* AAR Academy Series 60. Atlanta: Scholars, 1988.

Dyer, Richard. "Weiß," *Frauen und Film* 54/55 (1994) 65–80.

_____. *White.* London and New York: Routledge, 1997.

Giroux, Henry. "Racial Politics and the Pedagogy of Whiteness," in Mike Hill, ed., *Whiteness. A Critical Reader.* New York: New York University Press, 1997, 294–315.

Koch, Gertrud. *Die Einstellung ist die Einstellung: visuelle Konstruktionen des Judentums.* Frankfurt am Main: Suhrkamp, 1992.

Langford, Jacob. *Memory Mapping. An Essay on Time and Power.* Berlin, 1998.

Lippert, Renate. "'You make me feel like a natural woman.' Konstruktionen 'weißer' Weiblichkeit in Vom Winde verweht," *Frauen und Film* 54/55 (1994) 95–111.

Roediger, David. *The Wages of Whiteness. Race and the Making of the American Working Class.* London and New York: Verso, 1991.

Schilson, Arno. *Medienreligion. Zur religiösen Signatur der Gegenwart.* Tübingen: Francke, 1997.

Schlüpmann, Heide. "Jalousie. Zu William Wylers 'The Letter,'" *Frauen und Film* 54/55 (1994) 81–93.

Ulrike Metternich

"Dynamis and Womanpower."
An Investigation of the Concept of *dynamis*
in the Gospels and Paul

"Something always emerges when you work with biblical texts. You just have to ask the right questions." Thus Luise Schottroff encouraged us women and men in the doctoral seminar. And she was right. Each of us, on her or his journey of investigation, made completely unexpected new discoveries—discoveries and results that at the beginning of a dissertation were unknown to any of us. Sometimes to our own astonishment we found pieces of gold in the stream of biblical tradition, deeply hidden under the gravel of traditional biblical exegesis. One such gold piece for me is the concept of *dynamis* (power/strength). Here I want to give a report of my journey of discovery and tell how I came across this word, how I turned it and examined it from all sides, and how on closer inspection it came to seem to me more and more valuable, almost like a hidden treasure resting, forgotten, in the chest of tradition.

Mark 5:25-34

A woman who has suffered from genital bleeding for twelve years approaches Jesus from behind and touches his cloak because she thinks: "If I but touch his clothes, I will be made well." She senses a power coursing through her body. She knows that she is healed. Jesus also senses the power that has gone out of him, and he looks around for the one who touched him. She stands before him. She knows what has happened to her. She tells him the whole truth.

What kind of power was it that flowed between Jesus and the woman when she touched him? Is this a superstitious notion, or a kind of popular magical idea of the time (as many commentaries say)? Is it a typical element of a miracle story that we can now wave off with a tolerant smile? I don't think that it is.

121

The Greek word for the power that courses between Jesus and the woman is *dynamis*. *Dynamis* is far more than a miraculous event. *Dynamis* is strength, power, effect that flows out of a person. In what follows I prefer not to translate the word *dynamis* because every translation is at the same time an interpretation that attaches a particular meaning. Besides, we also use words like "dynamic" in English, and its associations, such as movement, energy, emanation are an appropriate background against which to approach the field of meaning of *dynamis* in the biblical writings.

Dynamis in the Synoptic Gospels

If we hold our bucket in the flowing river of the New Testament tradition the word *dynamis* will swim into it 119 times, 35 of them in the synoptic gospels. I would like to select a few examples out of the total of these passages. In the synoptic tradition *dynamis* is not a static concept; it refers to a vital effectiveness, a state of being filled by the divine presence. God's *dynamis* transforms, creates something new, puts in motion. Thus Mary is promised by the angel that she will conceive a child through the effective presence of the Holy Spirit and the "*dynamis* of the Most High" (Luke 1:35).

When Jesus comes preaching, people ask in astonishment: "Where did he get this wisdom and *dynamis*?" (Mark 6:2, *par.* Matt 13:54). *Dynamis* appears as divine energy that is visible through Jesus and so can be experienced by others. The synoptic authors regularly describe what Jesus does with the plural form of *dynamis* as *dynameis*, deeds in which the work of God is present. But Jesus is not the only one in possession of *dynamis*. He gives "*dynamis* and authority" to all his disciples as they go out to preach and to heal (Luke 9:1). At the end of the Gospel of Luke it is the Risen One who promises that "*dynamis* from on high" will be poured out on all believers (Luke 24:49). Thus in the gospels *dynamis* is an important, positive concept that names the invisible but clearly sensed activity of divine power.

Dynamis is thus also a concept applied to a liminal experience. God's power is at work in the midst of existing realities to transform them. Nevertheless, this power of God is not obvious or superficial. It depends on whether people open themselves to it, surrender to it. But those who sense it will have their eyes opened. They stand up, set themselves in motion; they are freed for a new life. It is as Isaiah prophesied: "Then the eyes of the blind shall be opened, and the ears of the deaf unstopped; then the lame shall leap like a deer, and the tongue of the speechless sing for joy" (Isa 35:5-6a). Perhaps there is no other way to speak of this power of God than to say: "I have experienced it."

Dynamis: A Wholistic Experience

Mark 5:25-34 and parallels recount the *dynamis*-experience of the woman with a hemorrhage. This story has a narrative form that is unusual in the New Testament. The thoughts of the woman and Jesus are detailed much more fully than in other stories. I am convinced that this is not incidental, the application of a fixed form, but rather it is indispensably necessary for the depiction of *dynamis. Dynamis* is mentioned here for the first time in Mark's gospel. The narrative, which at first sight appears to be a miracle story, reveals itself on closer inspection as a text full of highly-charged theological concepts. It is about faith, salvation, peace, truth, and power. The fact that the woman touches Jesus is far more than a sign of naïve superstition.

This scene recalls the promise in Zech 8:23, where it is said of the time of salvation: "In those days ten men from nations of every language shall take hold of a Jew, *grasping his garment* and saying, 'Let us go with you, for we have heard that God is with you.'" The woman with the hemorrhage does exactly what people will do if they sense Jesus' *dynamis* and realize: "God is with you." The touch is therefore also a prophetic sign. But it does not remain merely an external sign. As she touches, *dynamis* courses through the woman's whole body. The effects of the *dynamis* are, for the woman, a divine encounter. She is filled with fear and trembling (Mark 5:33), just as the women tremble at Jesus' empty tomb (Mark 16:8). The woman knows what has happened to her. She tells Jesus "the whole truth" (Mark 5:33). Being grasped by the power of God has made her a daughter of the reign of God. She is one of the saved. Therefore her *dynamis*-experience has a present-eschatological dimension. In this moment, for her, "the time is fulfilled, and the reign of God has come near" (Mark 1:15). Her experience confirms and expands the growth of the reign of God among humans.

Dynamis in Paul

Paul uses the concept of *dynamis* 36 times, about as often as the three synoptic gospels together. Using some selected examples from his letters, I want to make it clear that Paul also uses the word *dynamis* to describe the work of divine power. Thus in 1 Cor 2:3-5 he writes: "I came to you in weakness and in fear and in much trembling. My speech and my proclamation were not with plausible words of wisdom, but with a demonstration of the Spirit and of power *(dynamis)*, so that your faith might rest not on human wisdom but on the power *(dynamis)* of God."

Like the woman in Mark 5:25-34 and parallels, Paul reveals himself as a person who speaks with "fear and trembling," one driven by God's power. His whole striving is for the goal of making God's *dynamis* perceptible. Just as, after Jesus has spoken, people rise up in astonishment and ask "where did he get his *dynamis?*" so Paul also hopes that God's *dynamis* will reach people's hearts through his speaking. For as Paul knows, faith does not rest on eloquence, but on the *dynamis* of God. Faith is not abstract knowledge, the acceptance as true of finely honed phrases. Faith is being seized, touched by the effective presence of God. Faith is founded on the lived experience of *dynamis,* which opens heart and mind for a new reality in the midst of the realities that already exist. The reign of God is coming. It lives where people are moved by the power of God. For Paul, that power of God is an effective reality. Even in situations of extreme danger he praises God, who says: "My . . . power *(dynamis)* is made perfect in weakness" (2 Cor 12:9). In this sense Paul can write in 1 Cor 4:20: "the reign of God is [or depends] not in [on] talk *(logos)* but in [on] power *(dynamis)."*

For me this opens a new horizon of understanding. Not in Logos, but in *dynamis* is God's reign growing among us. I grew up in a theological tradition in which the word was central. I have heard and read a great many words. But if I understand Paul correctly here and consider the working of *dynamis,* a new challenge must be posed to this flood of words. The question is: where is *dynamis* at work? Does it live from words, from talk, from preaching, from works of help and healing?

Apparently there is a deeply-rooted biblical tradition of speaking about God's power as a *dynamis* to be experienced. The women in Mark 5:25-34 and parallels sensed it. For Paul also it was the experience of *dynamis* that set him in motion. I believe that it would be worthwhile to reflect anew on this little-appreciated but central theological concept. We today can understand what the word *dynamis* intends to express, for the workings of *dynamis* extend even to the present day.

Women Full of *Dynamis*

For me, *dynamis* is active today as well. In my life women especially, though not exclusively, have caused me to sense the *dynamis* of their faith. These are women in whom I have seen: here is dynamism, here is life, here are dreams and visions that move me. They are women who draw me out of my hopelessness and resignation, give me courage to stand up, break out, and trust in this invisible, but vividly perceptible power of God. Such women are for me "powerful women" in the best sense of the word—women who, like the woman with the hemorrhage, speak "the whole truth" today, women whose knowledge and skill are often scarcely recognized or are even deliberately repressed by the male disciples. They are women who are transgressors, trespassers on a pilgrimage between resignation and hope, who nevertheless do not despair because they repeatedly draw strength from the power of biblical visions.

For me Luise Schottroff is one of them. I frequently recall a conversation in the doctoral seminar when we were discussing the manifold problems of our own time. In discouragement, I said: "When I see how much there is to do, I often feel so powerless." Luise Schottroff answered spontaneously: "If you feel powerless, they have you just where they want you." Without *dynamis* we are playthings in the hands of the powerful. But having faith means sensing the power of God in oneself. Faith rests on the experience that even when we feel powerless God's power sustains us. Whoever lives from *dynamis* is living, in motion, treasuring hope, countering the power plays of the ruling powers. Whoever lives from *dynamis* is daughter and son in the reign of God, worker in God's vineyard, transgressive trespasser crossing the boundary between heaven and earth. Paul says of such people that they will be "a demonstration of the Spirit and of power *(dynamis)*" (1 Cor 2:4b).

I would like to close my essay with a prayer for *dynamis* that I wrote for a worship service:

> O God, source of our strength, fill us anew and
> give us the power to reconcile where there is conflict,
> give us the power to do justice where we see injustice,
> give us the power to speak the right word where it is needed,
> give us the power to say goodbye, so that we can let go with confidence,
> give us the power of new beginnings, so that we may sustain hope,
> give us the power for friendship, so that we may live gladly,
> give us the power we need for each new day.
>
> Amen.

Bibliography

Batmartha (Petermann), Ina Johanne. "Machen Geburt und Monatsblutung die Frau 'unrein'? Zur Revisionsbedürftigkeit eines mißverstandenen Diktums," in Luise Schottroff and Marie-Theres Wacker, eds., *Von der Wurzel getragen. Christlich-feministische Exegese in Auseinandersetzung mit Antijudaismus.* Leiden, New York, and Cologne: Brill, 1996, 43–60.

Feld, Geburgis. "'. . . wie es eben Frauen ergeht.' (Gen 31,35). Kulturgeschichtliche Überlegungen zum gegenwärtigen Umgang mit der Menstruation der Frau in Gesellschaft und Theologie," in ibid., 29–42.

Kahl, Brigitte. "Jairus und die verlorenen Töchter Israels. Sozio-literarische Überlegungen zum Problem der Grenzüberschreitung in Mk 5,21-43," in ibid., 61–78.

Martina S. Gnadt

"What we will be has not yet been revealed." An Archaeology of Seeing in John 9

Looks are open, questioning, crafty, furtive, challenging, humiliating, encouraging, far-seeing, defenseless, bitter. They build bridges, encounter one another, destroy, kill. Looks get under your skin. They touch your heart. Looks *do* something. They shape and change what "is"—depending on your perspective. Looks are like mirrors. We see the "other" brokenly; brokenly, we recognize ourselves in their eyes. Theology is always concerned that this brokenness not be forgotten, that what is ambiguous and preliminary not be regarded as clear and final. "'I' is an other" (Rimbaud). Seeing life, "the Other," and oneself in this way means *paying attention* to one's own and others' limitations, separations, exclusions, always seeing them as tentative and questionable, and keeping one's eyes open for what is new and what is coming into being.

I invite readers to this way of transgressing, of walking the line, and I am eager to try it through the eyes of John 9.

Looking Through the Eyes of Jesus' Disciples

The story in John 9 begins with looks: Jesus and his disciples pass by and see a man who was born blind. They stop. What the disciples see evokes questions: "Rabbi, who sinned, this man or his parents, that he was born blind?" What do they see, these who ask that quesiton, and what does their question say about their looking? According to the traditional interpretation the disciples' view is shaped by the notion of a direct connection between deed and consequence. For the disciples, blindness is a punishment from God. They ask who is guilty. This view, identified by interpreters as genuinely Jewish, Jesus rejects absolutely (Bultmann 1959). If we follow this direction in interpreting the disciples' seeing, it is unnecessary or even forbidden for us as Christians

127

to spend much time on the disciples' question. It is a non-question. Its *Jewish* view is out of date, false.

There are reasons for not following that direction. It is true that there was a rabbinic discussion within Judaism in which one side held that birth defects were traceable to improper sexual behavior by the parents *(Nedarim)*. It is possible to understand the disciples' question against that background (for what follows cf. Schottroff 1997). But it is not representative for *Judaism*, as is usually insinuated (Billerbeck 1961, 2:529). In the discussion referred to, the contrary opinion, corresponding to Jesus' answer, was also defended. Against this background the disciples' question appears Jewish, but not *typically* Jewish, and Jesus' answer sets him at odds with one position, but not at odds with *Judaism*. I understand the disciples' question and Jesus' answer as belonging to an internal Jewish controversy in which different perspectives were enunciated. I want to examine this controversy more closely, beginning with the disciples. What do they see when they look at the blind man at the side of the road? What does their question say about their view?

First of all: the disciples concentrate their attention on this man and ask questions. His fate disturbs them. They see blindness and speak of sin. How should we understand that connection?—in the sense of an equation of deed and consequence? Sickness as punishment for sexual misconduct? God as a punisher who allows children to be born with handicaps because the parents have offended against a particular sexual morality? Or can we posit another interpretation of sin as background to the disciples' question, one that does not equate sin with sexual misbehavior and does not regard sickness as punishment for such acts?

I find this other, non-moralistic Jewish interpretation of sin, for example, in Psalm 38 (see the further examples in Krobath and Schottroff 1991; cf. also Schaumberger and Schottroff 1988). The person who prays this psalm laments bitterly over his or her misery: she or he is powerless and shattered, with no soundness of body; the light of her or his eyes has gone out. This person's loved ones and friends have abandoned her or him, and the opponents threaten on every side. The lament over the individual's "sin" or entanglement (v. 4, *ḥatta:* injury to the community relationship between people and between people and God) is written within this all-comprehending situation of suffering. "Sin" is part of the burden of suffering (v. 5, *ʿwonotai:* "my iniquities . . . weigh like a burden too heavy for me") under which the one praying is almost crushed. Acknowledgment of guilt and sorrow for it (v. 19) are also part of the experience of suffering. Sickness, abandonment, persecution, and one's own guilty entanglement—the one praying spreads this whole complex of misery before God in order to cry out to God for help.

Against this background of sin as a guilty entanglement in an all-encompassing, oppressive context of suffering I hear the disciples asking: "Who sinned?" They know that the experience of guilt is part of the whole experience of suffering because people are never merely victims of circumstance. They are always involved. That means that being guilty is as much a part of life as contributing to one's own success. The disciples see that connection between guilt and the burden of suffering when they look at the blind man. But their view is different from that of the one who prays Psalm 38. While he or she, in lamenting before God, looks at the whole of her or his misery and thus is entirely present to the thing to which he cries to God for help, the disciples cast their eyes backward and away from themselves: "Who sinned, this man or his parents?" They look for the causes of this suffering, or the persons who caused it. The actual life of the blind man does not come into their question, nor do they themselves. They behold the blind man; they even pause, but their look remains distanced. They isolate the question of guilt from the question of suffering. They seek an explanation, not help. Their look is turned backward, not really toward the one who sits there before them.

Jesus' Look

Jesus also saw the man born blind, observed him even before the disciples posed their question. What did he see? What did his answer say about his view? "Neither this man nor his parents sinned; he was born blind so that God's works might be revealed in him." As a rule these words of Jesus are seen as a strict rejection of the either-or of the disciples, a sign that Jesus did not enter into that common discussion, but instead referred strictly to this single case. God's works are to be revealed in this blind man: thus Jesus' words point forward to the healing miracle (Bultmann 1959, 251). The problem, that the blind man had to endure years of suffering so that, in the end, God could reveal divine power through him, did not cross the mind of the narrator (Haenchen 1980, 377). This look from Jesus, as reconstructed by the exegetes, functionalizes the blind man, making him an object of demonstration to fulfill another purpose. His healing is a demonstration of the fullness of divine power; the blind man is a replaceable, expedient object; Jesus' look is distanced, because it is really aimed at a "higher object." I see points in Jesus' answer and in the progress of the story that cause me to undertake a critical review of this reconstruction of Jesus' looking.

"Neither this man nor his parents sinned" (v. 3a). Jesus explicitly says that the man is not guilty of sin. He does not see in him a person entangled in sin, as the disciples do, even though he understands the connection between sin and sickness (cf. John 5:14). Instead, he sees a person in need whom God wants to help. He refers to that help: "that God's works might be revealed in him" (v. 3b). Jesus draws attention to the help that is close to the blind man (cf. Ps 38:21-22 [MT 22-23]). It is this *help* that he sees when he looks at the man born blind; he looks at it, too. This is a look that sees good things coming when suffering springs to the eye. It is an expectant look. "God will help this person." Jesus' look is forward, to the future, not backward like that of the disciples. I see in this shift of perspective the distinction Jesus draws over against the disciples. It is a matter of the vanishing point from which the blind man is observed: it is *before* him, not behind him. It is in the presence of God's help and not in that of his or his parents' guilt.

There are traditions in the Hebrew Bible about God's seeing: above all Exod 3:7-8: "I have observed the misery of my people who are in Egypt; I have heard their cry on account of their taskmasters. Indeed, I know their sufferings, and I have come down to deliver them from the Egyptians, and to bring them up out of that land to a good and broad land." This is a seeing that brings salvation and opens a future. It is a partisan look that perceives the extent of suffering and injustice, full of solidary union with the miserable and the oppressed; it is a look that opens a future where in truth hopeless misery rules. That God's help is near in oppressive situations and makes possible something new is attested by traditions like Isa 29:17-19: "Shall not Lebanon in a very little while become a fruitful field, and the fruitful field be regarded as a forest? On that day the deaf shall hear the words of a scroll, and out of their gloom and darkness the eyes of the blind shall see. The meek shall obtain fresh joy in the LORD, and the neediest people shall exult in the Holy One of Israel." God's future is for the despairing hearts: "Say to those who are of a fearful heart, 'Be strong, do not fear! Here is your God. He will come with vengeance, with terrible recompense. He will come and save you.' Then the eyes of the blind shall be opened, and the ears of the deaf unstopped; then the lame shall leap like a deer, and the tongue of the speechless sing for joy. For waters shall break forth in the wilderness, and streams in the desert" (Isa 35:4-6). God sees misery and comes to help. God sees and comforts and creates justice. God looks at the blind, seeing them into sight; God sees the speechless into speech, the lame into leaping. God's look, taking sides and helping, turned forward, opens opportunities for life that previously were closed.

I understand Jesus' look within the horizon of God's seeing. Jesus sees the man born blind and also the help that is close to him. It is a look to the future. The other important aspect of Jesus' response is that he includes himself and the disciples in this helping way of seeing that is God's. Thus he overcomes the distance reflected in the disciples' seeing: "We must work the works of him who sent me while it is day; night is coming when no one can work. As long as I am in the world, I am the light of the world" (John 9:4-5). The disciples are included in his "we." They are no longer questioning observers, but are declared to be cooperating actors: "*We* must. . . ." The urgency in these words is also evident: help is needed right away. In this I see a reference to the pressing situation of the blind man. Even though he has been blind for such a long time he urgently needs help. Therefore Jesus begins immediately (cf. the continuation with *tauta eipōn* in v. 6).

"When he had said this, he spat on the ground and made mud with the saliva and spread the mud on the man's eyes" (v. 6). The traditional interpretation removes itself from this scene in a twofold way. On the one hand it subordinates the action to the word, which serves for it as an illustration of Jesus' saying about light (Haenchen 1980, 378). Jesus' words are decisive; the gesture, thus understood, is only an incidental addition. On the other hand, in the eyes of the interpreters Jesus' action is also distant, material, medicinal (Gnilka 1983, 76). The "crassly material method of healing" is said to be surprising (Haenchen 1980, 378). On the contrary, I see the real weight of the healing scene within the context of the story. It is not a mere illustration of the saying about light, but an independent element. Jesus' look is applied to the need through, and only through, his action. I also observe how close Jesus comes to the blind man. A look can be distant, but Jesus' action is not. He spreads some of his own saliva, mixed with dirt, on the sensitive parts of the blind man's eyes. Saliva can be injurious, for example when it strikes someone in the face, as happened, according to Matthew's gospel, in Jesus' Passion (Matt 26:67; 27:30). The Fourth Gospel speaks of Jesus' being struck in the face, not spat upon (John 19:3). That may be connected to this healing function in John 9. The gesture of spitting achieves its clear meaning only in the concrete situation, as here in the eye contact of Jesus and the man born blind: they come close to one another as only people who trust each other can do. Jesus' look achieves effectiveness through his action. The help he saw in prospect is now palpable; the disciples' distance is now overcome in a physical sense.

Shifting Perspectives

"'Go, wash in the pool of Siloam' (which means Sent)" (v. 7a). The blind man is not yet healed. Jesus' action is the beginning of the healing. Then the story describes the blind man's actions: "Then he went and washed and came back able to see" (v. 7). At this point a change of perspective occurs *within* the story: to this point the blind man was seen only as reflected in the eyes of the disciples and Jesus. Now for the first time he determines the action by himself; he himself becomes active. He does what Jesus tells him. I see in this correspondence (between v. 7a and v. 7b) not so much the perfect obedience of the blind man, *subordinate* to Jesus' words (Barrett 1990, 360) as the *cooperation* of the two. It is true that Jesus takes the initiative in the healing without asking the sick man, but it is only the blind man's action that completes the healing. "The narrator is not interested in how the blind man finds his way to the pool of Siloam." With this laconic observation Haenchen (1980, 378) dismisses the blind man's action. I do not share the ignorant glance of interpreters at the blind man and his action, which "overlooks" this fundamental shift in perspective within the story. Instead, I want to look still more closely at this "moment" between the blind man's departure and his return, seeing. Can we find within it the perspective of the man born blind on what he is experiencing?

The Look of the Man Born Blind

"Then he went and washed and came back able to see." The blind man cannot see the way he is going. And his goal? What he will be has not yet appeared. The passage of the man born blind from the world of the blind to the world of the seeing is a uniquely in-between state. For a while he remains on the border between the two worlds. He becomes a trespasser, walking the line (cf. Luther 1992, 212ff.) between the old order of his life and the new that does not yet exist. How has he lived heretofore? I am asking, in terms of social history, about the conditions of the life of a person like this, shaped from birth by his disability. He is one of the many people who cannot feed themselves through the work of their hands, not even as day-laborers. He is dependent—physically, economically, and socially. He begs (v. 14) and depends on the help and mercy of other people. Economically he is among the poorest of the poor.

However, I do not want to describe the blind man's situation one-sidedly as something entirely negative, seeing him solely as the victim of his suffering, thus stigmatizing him all over again through my observation. Being born blind means a drastic restriction of possibilities from many points of view. However, even a hard fate like that is not just gloomy misery, not only isolation and impoverishment. The neighbors in particular support this point of view when they debate about the healed blind man. Their discussion is described in remarkable detail (vv. 8-9). This note is socio-historically significant because it attests to the interest that the blind beggar arouses in those around him. He is not completely isolated; instead, his healing causes comment. He has his place in society. He is known in the neighborhood; he sits on the edge of the road, visible, in public. Now he leaves his place. He stands up, goes to the pool of Siloam, and washes himself. Note: he is not yet healed. He does these things *as a blind man.* He hears and understands what Jesus says to him; he is not lame; he finds the way and can wash himself. "The narrator is not interested in how the blind man finds his way to the pool of Siloam." This assertion of Haenchen's comes up short. The narrators are indeed interested that the blind man should find the way, both there and back again, that he is in a position to follow Jesus' urging independently and responsibly. The blind man does not appear here as helpless and dependent, but as an independently acting person. Jesus addresses him in terms of what he can do, and that is anything but incidental; it is exactly what helps him to come to his healing. At this important point the blind man is different from the lame man at the pool of Beth-zatha, who could not help himself (John 5:1-9). While at the beginning of the story the blind man was present only as reflected in the eyes of Jesus and the disciples, he now comes directly into view. While at the beginning his blindness was the center of interest and the occasion for a question, now his handicap retreats behind his ability to play an active role in his healing. While previously the observations of the others, the seeing persons, dominated, now the perspective of this person, who is blind *and* finds his way, comes into effect (differently Wilhelm 1998).

This perspective, which places the man born blind in the middle, becomes still more sharply focused in the course of the story: first when, after his healing, he responds to the the puzzled questions of the neighbors about his identity with "I am the man" (v. 9). The one who has been the subject of discussion for such a long time now speaks for himself. Interestingly enough, it is his ability to see that is taken by the seeing people as a deviation from the norm, and that provokes questions: "Is it he or not?" The neighbors ask about the one they know, the one who is familiar to them. Their look seeks the continuity that has been called into question by the passage of this trespasser from not-seeing to being-able-to-see. "I am the man." With this answer the "connection" is achieved: the one healed is the one born blind, as the neighbors know him, but at the same time the one born blind is now one who sees. There is continuity in discontinuity. The one who walked the line has now become one who crosses over, leaving the old behind. "I am the man"—I am the one you know. At the same time it is true that "I went and washed and received my sight." We should not undervalue the fact that the voice of the man born blind is now clearly heard. With a knowing look he testifies to those who were not present about how he came to see, and what role he played in the result. We learn still more about that look in the course of the story, as yet another group enters the picture: the Pharisees.

The Looking of the Pharisees

One can read in the looks of the Pharisees some quite different things, for they are anything but uniform as a group. "Some of the Pharisees" (v. 16), who have listened to the blind man's repeated description, judge Jesus: "This man is not from God, for he does not observe the sabbath." With this judgment they simultaneously formulate the question that concerns them as regards Jesus: Is he from God, or not? In this context one's judgment of the healing is also in question: Is it from God or not? These Pharisees think that the Sabbath commandment has been broken in the healing of the man born blind. One very frequently encounters in exegesis of this passage references to the Jewish interpretation in *m. Šab.* 7.2, according to which kneading dough—and consequently Jesus' "questionable manipulation" (Bultmann 1959, 252) —would be forbidden on the Sabbath. It is said that Jesus set himself above the Sabbath or even that he abolished the "Law" altogether (Barrett 1990, 364). The story itself shows that the question "from God or not?" was hotly discussed: "But other [Pharisees] said, 'How can a man who is a sinner perform such signs?'" (v. 16). For some the Sabbath commandment, as they interpret it, forbids healing. They see Jesus as someone who transgresses this commandment and thus despises the will of God. For the others the healing is a visible proof in which they see that Jesus follows the Sabbath commandment as they understand it, and fulfills the will of God.

These different positions represent two different ways of looking at the Sabbath commandment and the healing event. Their difference and incompatibility are seen and appreciated: "And they were divided" (v. 16)—another internal Jewish controversy. The acerbity of the argument is explained by the importance of what is at stake. Ultimately it is a question of Jewish identity. The struggle over the Sabbath commandment is not the expression of legalism, such as is often attributed to Judaism, but rather the expression of concern for the Jewish way (*halakhah*), which must continually be rediscovered and which is maintained through keeping the Torah. Is it in accordance with God's will for this man born blind to be healed on the Sabbath? (cf. Müller 1997). The story is apparently on the side of those who give an affirmative answer to this question, as does the healed man himself. His look is shown here also, in this central question about his healing, to be understanding and knowledgeable. The relationship between Jesus and the man born blind has been reversed: while previously Jesus had his eye on the man born blind, now we learn something about the man born blind's view of Jesus. He takes his side, affirms him as one who does the works of God, believes him and kneels before him (v. 38).

"What we will be has not yet been revealed."

The first letter of John, from which this quotation comes, continues: "What we do know is this: when he is revealed, we will be like him [God], for we will see him as he is" (1 John 3:2). This is a word of hope that holds open both our own identity and that of God, but without falling into indistinctness: "we are God's children now" (3:2a). I think the look of the man born blind directed at Jesus, at himself and at his healing, is to be located precisely at this nodal point between "already" and "not yet." "From God"—this judgment by the man born blind, now seeing, means: What has happened here is *good* in a deep, soothing sense. That is not clear to all participants; it remains ambiguous. But in the judgment of the one healed it is utterly clear, as it is for all who follow his view. It is good, and it is good now. The healing has a special quality. Over it stands the name of God. And with this a second matter is addressed: The horizon of what has happened here—in Jesus' action and that of the man born blind—is very broad. It is a horizon of hope that promises a *good* aim for the whole people of Israel: "On that day the deaf shall hear the words of a scroll, and out of their gloom and darkness the eyes of the blind shall see. The meek shall obtain fresh joy in the LORD, and the neediest people shall exult in the Holy One of Israel" (Isa 29:18-19).

The future is painted in recurring images of healing: "Then the eyes of the blind shall be opened, and the ears of the deaf unstopped; then the lame shall leap like a deer, and the tongue of the speechless sing for joy" (Isa 35:5-6). The non-human creation is also included: "For waters shall break forth in the wilderness, and streams in the desert" (Isa 35:6b). The story of the man born blind is inscribed within this broad eschatological horizon of Israel's hope: "from God" ties the concrete healing of *this* person to the yet-awaited healings of those who are still sitting at the side of the road. Between "already" and "not yet" the blind-born trespasser praises God who has already helped him, God whom Jesus saw coming, God whose coming to help is still awaited.

The horizon opened by the look of the man born blind is very broad; it includes all those who, sitting at the side of the road, are in need of God's help, and for whom the story of the man born blind who now sees awakens hope—hope that God's look that comes to our aid *comes to engage* boundaries, so that what is not yet possible will indeed become possible. "'I' is an other," or, as the look of the man born blind expresses it: "what we will be has not yet been revealed."

Bibliography

Barrett, Charles Kingsley. *The Gospel according to St John: An Introduction with Commentary and Notes on the Greek Text.* London: S.P.C.K., 1958.

Billerbeck, Paul, and Hermann L. Strack. *Kommentar zum Neuen Testament aus Talmud und Midrasch.* 6 vols. in 7. Munich: Beck, 1922–1961.

Bultmann, Rudolf. *Das Evangelium des Johannes.* 16th ed. Göttingen: Vandenhoeck & Ruprecht, 1959. English: *The Gospel of John; A Commentary.* Translated by G. R. Beasley-Murray. Oxford: B. Blackwell; Philadelphia: Westminster, 1971.

Gnilka, Joachim. *Johannesevangelium.* NEB 4. Würzburg: Echter, 1983.

Haenchen, Ernst. *Das Johannesevangelium: ein Kommentar.* Tübingen: Mohr, 1980. English: *John: A Commentary on the Gospel of John.* Translated by Robert W. Funk. Hermeneia. Philadelphia: Fortress, 1984.

Krobath, Evi, and Luise Schottroff. "Sünde/Schuld III. Feministisch-theologische Diskussion. Neues Testament," in Elisabeth Gössmann et al., eds., *Wörterbuch der feministischen Theologie.* Gütersloh: Gerd Mohn, 1991, 385–87.

Luther, Henning. *Religion und Alltag. Bausteine zu einer praktischen Theologie des Subjekts.* Stuttgart: Radius, 1992.

Müller, Stefanie. "'Ist der Sabbat für den Menschen geschaffen?' Zum jüdischen Sabbatverständnis (Mk 2,23-28)," in Dagmar Henze, et al., *Antijudaismus im Neuen Testament? Grundlagen für die Arbeit mit biblischen Texten.* Gütersloh: Chr. Kaiser, 1997, 114–25.

Schaumberger, Christine, and Luise Schottroff. *Schuld und Macht. Studien zu einer feministischen Befreiungstheologie.* Munich: Kaiser, 1988.

Schottroff, Luise. "Sexualität im Johannesevangelium," *EvTh* 5 (1997) 437–44.

Wilhelm, Dorothee. "Wer heilt hier wen? Und vor allem: wovon? Über biblische Heilungsgeschichten und andere Ärgernisse," *Schlangenbrut.* Thematic issue: "Sehnsucht nach Heilung," 62 (1998) 10–12.

Hanna Kreisel-Liebermann

Protecting and Holding: Pastoral Companionship for Cancer Patients in a Multidisciplinary Team

Quality of Life in the Face of Death

The diagnosis "cancer" is a shock for everyone. Our plans for our life are acutely challenged. The diagnosis sweeps like the shadow of death through all those affected by it: in Germany, statistically, every fourth person (Husebø and Klaschik 1998, 1). But the end is not near for every one of them.

Since January 1998 I have been part of a team of two nurses and two doctors who accompany women and men who are not far from the end of their lives and suffer from painful tumors. The task of the palliative care team (PCT) in Project SUPPORT is to be companions to ambulant patients, to ease pain, to control symptoms, and to give both psychosocial and pastoral support. The quality of life of these patients is to be secured in a situation in which life has frequently become nothing but torture. Quality of life means especially that they do not lose their own voices, and that even as sick people they remain respected fellow human beings, people who are taken seriously. It is desirable that they remain at home, in their familiar surroundings, embedded in daily life. This is possible when friends or relatives are willing to spend the time and strength needed to help them. It is amazing what some spouses and life partners do. At home, or in a hospice when nothing else is possible any longer, or in a palliative care station, the final phase of life can be lived intensively. Whenever possible, wishes are fulfilled that may seem eccentric from a clinical standpoint but are quite natural from a human standpoint: for example, a visit to the theater, a trip to the beach, or going to the hairdresser. Quality of life can mean not being alone in one's illness, but remaining integrated in familial and social relationships. Quality of life also means having one or more people who offer professional care: doctors, caregivers, pastoral workers, psychologists. The purpose of the project is to discover what is necessary to secure quality of life in this situation: what kind of framework and what skills must be available to shape the final phase of life with dignity and autonomy?

"I can't bear it . . ."

Pain is a sign that there is a disturbance in the body. It signals: I am wounded, in soul or body. Feeling pain is a necessary experience: to put an end to pain we must be active, that is, seek for its causes and undertake therapy. Because pain cannot be measured from outside, but is experienced individually, the World Health Organization has developed an aid. The Visual Analog Scale is a sliding rule, made primarily of cardboard, with numbers from 0 to 10 and a colored strip shaded from yellow to dark red. The number 0 and the color yellow represent a pain-free state, the number 10 the strongest pain one has ever experienced in one's own body. The sick person can use this scale to convey the strength of his or her pain. Tumor patients frequently have pain at level 10 until they have received good pain therapy. Such pain is unbearable; people can die from it. Nevertheless, a great many tumor patients in Germany suffer unnecessary pain. "Only 19% of tumor patients with pain requiring opiates receive an adequate dosage of morphine as long as they are ambulant" (Sohn and Zenz 1998, 10). The reasons for this desolate situation are, on the one hand, the poor education of medical students in pain therapy and, on the other hand, the aversion of many primary care physicians to prescribing opiates (ibid.). Pain in the unbearable categories can be combatted only with opiates, that is, preparations of opium. These drugs (mainly retarded long-phase morphine) must be taken regularly on schedule in order to achieve an almost pain-free, that is, normal status.

Germany, where medical research and care have achieved a very high standard, is still a developing country as far as pain therapy is concerned. This, among other things, makes clear what little prominence the quality of life of sick people has in the field of medical ethics. Patients who are no longer curable in the medical sense are frequently permitted to suffer.

Palliative Medicine: Protecting and Holding

A madonna with protecting mantle (in a 13th-century sculpture) shelters both adults and children beneath her cloak. She is said to provide protection against sickness (at that time, the Black Death) and against life's emergencies. *Palliare* is Latin for covering with a mantle. Palliative therapy has as its goal surrounding seriously ill people with a protecting mantle and giving them security in the last phase of their life. Those who no longer feel secure in their own bodies need something to hold on to. Palliative medicine begins where classic medicine, which for the most part sees death as its enemy, ceases. Instead of saying "we can't do anything more for you," it says "we can still do a lot for you," even if the illness is terminal. Palliative medicine means taking the rights of the sick and dying seriously; in Germany, as elsewhere, they are legally protected:

- The right to freedom (accepting or refusing medical treatment)
- The right to personal dignity and integrity (discretion)
- The right to information (diagnosis, therapy, prognosis)
- The right to appropriate treatment (including humane care)
- The right not to have to suffer
- The right not to have to die alone.

"A right is an option. The individual can decide for himself or herself whether he or she will claim the right or prefers to refuse it" (Husebø and Klaschik 1998, 295).

Palliative care is usually understood three-dimensionally: it includes medical, nursing, and psycho-social care. "The ethical bases of palliative care are grounded in the so-called hospice idea. . . . It accepts death as a normal process; it neither accelerates it nor lengthens it . . ." (ibid. 3). The mother of the hospice idea, dame Cecily Saunders, founded St. Christopher's Hospice in London thirty years ago. She said: "My task is to care for the patient's health. There are times when it is in the interest of health to die. It is not healthy to draw death out at length" (ibid. 35). Palliative companionship implies that dying is made easier, through all the means at hand: it is mercy, not making up someone else's mind for her or him.

Pastoral Care: Companionship in Life

"From the beginning, the hospice movement has regarded pastoral care as an important part of its work. . . . Being terminally ill, with a limited life expectancy, means having to take leave of people who mean a great deal to us. . . . The patient is confronted with the tasks of life that have been successfully completed and the scars that have been inflicted. Losses that were experienced in life are brought vividly to mind" (Husebø and Klaschik 1998, 288).

Pastoral care is *de facto* delivered in a cooperative multidisciplinary effort by doctors, caregivers, and professional pastoral workers. It is more accompaniment than care: it means leaving space for the sharing of fears, concerns, and feelings, leaving space for hope and for hopelessness. The eyes of seriously ill people are often like a cry for salvation. I can give space for the despair that speaks from their faces. To the question: "why did this happen to me?" I can render no answer. But we can talk about God: about God's helplessness and our desires for omnipotence.

Empathy is an important precondition for pastoral accompaniment. Empathy means attempting to feel with another human being, with all the organs of perception at our disposal and with alert interest to feel in company with the woman, man, or child who is willing to communicate with one. Knowing the limited time we will have with another requires the highest degree of honesty in both nonverbal and verbal communication. Accompaniment in life means regarding this phase of life as valuable, and valuing the person of the other to the last breath, and beyond.

Accepting one's own limitations is a precondition for communication with the most seriously ill people. Those who act as companions in this final phase bring much of their own strength, concentration, and empathy to the encounter in order to act well and helpfully. Frequently the members of the PCT experience an intensive presence with dying or seriously ill patients, lasting hours or recurring daily over a period of time, as hard work. Weariness and the need for rest signal the need to work through what has been experienced. "A dying process is sometimes a magnificent thing," said a nurse on the team. Just as mutual support in the team and supervision by an outsider are important, it is necessary that the members seek rest and relaxation. In the gospels we read that even Jesus frequently withdrew after healing people. In biblical stories of healing it is clear that the attention and empathy that produced healing works also exhausted Jesus. Restoration was accomplished through withdrawal (into the wilderness, to the opposite shore).

From January to September 1998 the Palliative Care Team accompanied 110 women and men aged 31 to 86, and one youth. Seventy of them died within those nine months. With most of them we experienced phases of great closeness as well as withdrawal. They had learned about pain: a torturing physical pain that was lowered and combated through the appropriate choice and application of medicines by the PCT doctors. The spiritual pain could only be worked through when the physical was under control. Each of the women and men we accompanied chose an individual way of doing that work.

Two women, Mrs. A (57) and Mrs. B (58) were treated by the Palliative Care Team for six months. At the beginning of our contact they were not obviously cancer-ridden or terminal. They were very disciplined, elegantly dressed, and despite repeated bouts of pain they were able to cover up their situation. Although they both knew that there were metastases throughout their bodies, Mrs. A always said: "I will not give up hope." Mrs. B emphasized: "All these years of struggle can't have been for nothing." Mrs. B had suffered through years of chemotherapy, with good periods in between, and had tried every kind of therapy that seemed to offer some hope. It was very important for her to have a conversation partner in the hospital who knew her path and her attitude: "I will make the decisions about my body." Even when she was confined to a wheelchair she still appeared quite healthy. In her little village, she said, her neighbors and friends would not believe that she was so sick. Although by this time she had had cancer for ten years, many people had said to her: "Oh, you'll be all right. You look wonderful." "Isn't it good," she said, "that people can't look inside you. But God knows how I look in there." She had always been the strong person in the family, and it was very difficult for her to give up that role. In pastoral conversations she was able to find a place in which to express her ambivalent feelings. She did not have to be the strong one and in my presence she could weep, something she did not permit herself in the presence of her family. She took time to tell me about the beautiful and the bitter times of her life. In this process she found a balance for herself.

Mrs. A was diagnosed with cancer twelve years ago. She, too, is an attractive woman who dresses with elegance and care. When I met her she was having difficulty walking, so she was often in her wheelchair. She had lost a lot of weight but that was not noticeable at first glance. She was racked with pain. When she had received a good balance of drugs she told me why she wanted to keep up her "façade," as she called it. She was separated from her husband and helped to care for her grandchildren, because her daughter was often overwhelmed. She built a house for the grandchildren. She did not want to burden her family, her children and grandchildren, but instead she wanted to be there for them "to the last breath." Only when her strength was utterly exhausted did she allow herself to be put in the hospital. A friend of hers was the head of the nursing station, and took loving care of her. Mrs. A did not want her grandchildren to visit her often. They were not to remember their (young) grandmother as so very sick. Always very charming, she was now quite aloof. "I can't afford to waste my strength," she said. She needed rest. She never spoke directly of death with me, but only in images: "That will be my last journey."

Mrs. B's husband was still in search of a new therapy. He asked the doctors in the team if they did not have something that could save his wife. It was difficult to walk the tightrope with him. The patient herself was too weak to use the telephone and did not want any more visitors. She knew that she, as she said, must probably look "the inevitable" in the face. Her husband could not and would not let go. His voice, his mood were uneasy and agitated. He could not bear to see that his wife was growing weaker and weaker. He cared for her and provided for her lovingly, but letting go was simply impossible for him.

Neither of these women could bear the dissolution of their bodies and did not want to be seen in that condition. It was hard for those who had cared for them before, whether physicians, nurses, or pastoral care workers, to bear it. It might have been helpful to tell them that we would not leave them alone, even and especially in the visible decline of their bodies.

Only a few of the patients I met in those nine months were ready to go. One older man, Mr. C (75), had found a way. He said: "Cancer is my constant companion. I can't do anything without him any more." Mr. C had a good sense of humor, and we laughed a lot together. He suffered because his wife could not deal with his weakness and lack of appetite. She had always cooked good food for him, and she wanted to give him the same care in this phase of his life. It came to be a source of conflict: she made his life difficult in their tiny apartment by cleaning and doing elaborate cooking, weeping all the while. We decided together that it would be better for both of them if he entered the hospice or palliative care station. It was a difficult step: both of them knew that he would never return home, but her pattern for daily life was so habitual that it did not seem possible for her to change and accommodate to the needs of the sick man. His wife visited him every day and always brought him something to eat. He was delighted. His wife told me later that she and her husband had never in their lives spent so much time together as since he had been sick. She was not used to it. Her husband, always agile, had worked hard and was always driving around in his car. When he became ill, he felt as if he were "in prison."

Mr. C needed some "free space" just as much as his wife did. He found it in the palliative care station, where he had as much care as he could bear. His wife was able to accompany her weakened and dying partner lovingly when he and she lived at some distance from each other.

These are three among many ways of living with serious disease and the approach of death. Mrs. A and Mrs. B had some things in common, and yet every way is different. Accompanying women and men a little way along this path has been a significant life experience for me. I have learned from them: even the last phase of life is part of the individual's biography. However, in our highly technologized country with its super-technological medicine it is not easy for people to shape this last time well. Still, rethinking has begun: since 1994 the German Society for Palliative Medicine is working as hard at initiatives for change as is the Hospice movement. Project SUPPORT is like a little grain sown, we hope, on fruitful ground.

Bibliography

Husebø, Stein B., and Eberhard Klaschik. *Palliativmedizin: Praktische Einführung in Schmerztherapie, Symptomkontrolle, Ethik und Kommunikation.* Heidelberg and Berlin: Springer, 1998.

Palliativeinheiten im Modellprogramm zur Verbesserung der Versorgung Krebskranker. Baden-Baden, 1997.

Sohn, Wolfgang, and Michael Zenz. *Morphinverschreibung in Europa.* Berlin and Heidelberg: Springer, 1998.

Andrea Bieler

Written in Their Bodies: On the Significance of Rituals in Caring for AIDS Patients[1]

People with HIV and AIDS are transgressors. In the church they represent a taboo zone in which themes of religion, sexuality, illness, and death are interwoven. They often live in milieus that are strange to the core communities of the local church. They are transgressors, trespassers because they bring before the eyes of the supposedly healthy what they are repressing in their own lives. In doing so, they set loose fears and raise defenses.

From my teacher Luise Schottroff I learned that it is essential for theology to look closely at what is happening on the boundaries, for that can be the place where the Word becomes flesh. The work of the Hamburg Pastorate for AIDS Care is for me an impressive example of what happens when rigid milieus are broken open, when boundaries become permeable, and when the transgressors lead us into the healing power of the Gospel that seizes both men and women.

The following essay is inspired by people who live in that community.

The Shifting Meaning of AIDS in the 1990s

Anyone with AIDS has no choice but to look imminent death in the face: in the 1980s AIDS quickly became a metaphor for death that comes on us in untimely fashion. Horrific descriptions in the media, which predicted early and massive numbers of dead and the expectation of an explosion of the numbers of HIV-infected people in the Federal Republic of Germany excited the population, who divided into

[1] I am especially grateful to Pastor Nils Christiansen for friendly and informative conversations about the work of the Pastorate for AIDS Care in Hamburg.

two camps: the liberals and the strict plague-police-oriented. In this phase the social discourse about AIDS was given over to features of a premodern image of illness. In 1989 Susan Sontag noted in this context a step backward into the past,

> before the era of medical triumphalism, when illnesses were innumerable, mysterious, and the progression from being seriously ill to dying was something normal (not, as now, medicine's lapse or failure, destined to be corrected). AIDS, in which people are understood as ill before they are ill; which produces a seemingly innumerable array of symptom-illnesses; for which there are only palliatives; and which brings to many a social death that precedes the physical one—AIDS reinstates something like a premodern experience of illness . . . (Sontag 1989, 34).

In contrast, the Protestant churches generally have abandoned premodern religious models of interpretation. Only a few understand AIDS as divine punishment or the expression of divine wrath. Still the ecclesiastical positions scarcely reflect any beginnings of critical self-reflection or readiness for repentance that could cause them to consider their own share in the stigmatization and exclusion of the various affected groups. Nevertheless, certain individual initiatives have been undertaken, for example the establishment of the Pastorate for AIDS Care in Hamburg, which encounters the stigmatized with respect and solidarity (cf. Jarchow 1996; Christiansen 1998).

At the same time a new culture of *ars moriendi* has become a challenge to which, in particular, people from the Gay movement and individual spiritual care projects have given impressive responses. In the course of time many of those affected have themselves become a kind of elite in dealing with the elementary themes of death and dying. The discovery of love that accepts the disgust and the other's fear of slow death and holds firm in its empathy has changed many people who act as companions to the dying. The memory of the dead, which, especially in the Protestant realm, finds only limited expression, has been given new forms. The distinctive individuality and dignity of each person and the equality of all people before God have found public expression in different worship services, public actions, and artistic projects. Washing and "waking" the dead have been rediscovered and make possible a physical-sensible comprehension of saying goodbye (cf. Christiansen and Höcker 1998). In this way the poverty of our culture of mourning, which surrenders the names of the dead and their life stories to oblivion, has been resisted. The recognition that the hope of resurrection can only be truly proclaimed in remembering the dead has taken concrete form: "The principle of hope freezes into icy cold;

hope for resurrection and eternal life is reversed to its contrary when it abandons sorrow, sorrow for the dead, the memory of their suffering" (Luther 1991, 420). What has happened on the fringes, in making sisters of sorrow and hope for resurrection, became an example for the popular church perspective as well.

At least since the World AIDS Conference at Vancouver in July 1996 the significance of the virus has been rewritten, at first with great euphoria: from now on it was a matter of a new perspective on life *with* AIDS. Through the development of new types of protease inhibitors and the antiretroviral combination therapies associated with them, which are able to hold dangerous opportunistic infections in check, the perspective on life had changed. Adjustment to death as the correct orientation of life gave way to the possibility of living with AIDS longer and better than previously expected. AIDS, so was the prognosis, was in the way of becoming a treatable, severe, chronic illness with which one can *live*. However, this development had its limitations. In the countries of southern Africa the AIDS epidemic devastated whole population groups, so that UN speakers no longer hesitate to make comparisons with the Black Death of the Middle Ages and the influenza pandemic of 1918 (cf. Kriener 1998, 3). In the United States and western Europe only those who were able to discipline their daily regime in terms of a rigid therapeutic plan could enjoy the blessings of the new medicines. As many as twenty-two pills a day had to be swallowed, before meals, after meals, some on an empty stomach, others combined with acidic fruit juices. A new word has appeared on the horizon: "therapeutic failure" is the title cynically assigned to those who have already developed resistance against certain drugs. The inevitable consequence of this development is the so-called "medicalization" of AIDS; the power of doctors and HMOs is again central, and there is danger that the psychosocial problems that accompany stigmatization will be accorded less importance.

As early as 1995 the speaker for the AIDS Association in Frankfurt, Stefan Majer, described the situation this way:

> This extension of survival is thus experienced both as the recovery of life's opportunities and also of *the things necessary for life*, and thus has quite ambivalent features. For death in the best years is also a rescue from the debilities of age; ending one's life in horror is a way of avoiding a life of unending horror. Thus no matter how much we desire victory over the AIDS-monster, at the same time we face the question of what kind of weapons we can bring against the monster. It is not only the successes of medicine, but also individual ability to resist and the coherence of the individual's concept of life, as well as the acceptance society offers to the affected person's

way of life, including his or her deviations and failures, that decide how much life can be wrung from AIDS. (Majer 1995, 4)

Daily life in the Pastorate for AIDS Care in Hamburg has also changed since the development of the new combined therapies. Accompanying sick people in the last phase of their lives and conscious preparation for funerals are no longer the major focus of our work. While up to the winter of 1996 we buried on average sixty-five people a year, since then the numbers have shrunk drastically. A change in perspective is in the making, and it is important for the Church's pastoral work as well. The task is now to wrest a new meaning from the situation of living with AIDS and to create a pastoral space in which the life stories of individuals can be told in the tension between new hopes for a future and the uncertainties that arise from treatments that still have feet of clay.

Transformation on the Borders:
Pastoral and Ritual-Theoretical Considerations

Pastoral workers who accompany people with HIV and AIDS report that many of their conversation partners have to struggle with truly archaic feelings of shame and uncleanness as regards their infection, feelings that are combined with a rejection of their own bodies and various forms of self-hatred. The experience of being somehow tainted inscribes itself in the body and affects one's whole sense of life and self-image. Mary Douglas has explained that ideas about pollution and taboo function as interpretations of the dominant viewpoint of the social order. In particular, offenses against the system of rules regarding contact with sexual secretions are inevitably threatened with punishment. Douglas represents the viewpoint "that ideas of separating, purifying, demarcating, and punishing transgressions have as their main function to impose system on an inherently untidy experience. It is only by exaggerating the difference between within and without, above and below, male and female, with and against, that a semblance of order is created" (Douglas 1966).

The portents of the discourse about normality and deviation, or purity and impurity with regard to socially disapproved forms of sexuality and the consumption of drugs and the associated taboo realms surrounding sexuality, religion, and death are likewise associated with ideas of dirt and soiling. They torment many people who have to live with HIV infection, in the tension between feelings of shame and guilt. The newly stabilized established-outsider configuration that comes with AIDS causes a great many to live with the experience of "standing on the other side of the bar" (Brix 1994, 19).

The introjection of such ideas leads to feelings of isolation and to those archaic interpretations of immunodeficiency disease in which illness is understood as a flooding of the body with unclean substances. The longing to be cleansed thus becomes a symbol for healing. This identification of healing with purification can be understood pastorally: what is needed is a separation of the ideal ego from the negative possession that AIDS connotes, so that the process of self-acceptance can be more powerfully enhanced. Only in this way can a moral rigorism in which the illness is seen as genuinely the consequence of an unclean action be averted. Thus pastoral care in this area has something to do with the unfolding of an exorcistic energy that can separate the individual from the demonically-experienced power of the images of reality so described. The power of the Gospel is here a power for separation.

If we are serious about the idea that pastoral care is essentially about understanding the life stories of individuals in the horizon of God's history with humanity, our concern for the portents that are inscribed in our bodies will not be dealt with solely in words. In this context rituals can be helpful in transforming the injured images of the self and the body. I take it as given that rituals effect a symbolic transformation of experience that "cannot be recognized through any clearer medium than that of formalized gesture" (Langer 1960).

This symbolic transformation is made possible by the liminality that attaches to rituals. Liminality (Latin *limen,* threshold) is to be understood as a threshold region in which passages between different periods of time, biographical phases, and heterogeneous symbolic worlds can be visibly engaged. Meaning is created at the place of passage. "Liminality is a temporal interface whose properties partially invert those of the already consolidated order which constitutes any specific cultural 'cosmos'" (Turner 1982, 41). This transition takes place, according to van Gennep's classic definition, in the three phases of separation, transition, and incorporation (cf. van Gennep 1909). In the first phase a clear separation between the sacred and profane spheres in the dimension of space and time is accomplished; daily routines are abandoned and preparation is made for the transformation. In the threshold space thus opened the participants pass through a stage of ambiguity in a social limbo that "has few (though sometimes these are most crucial) of the attributes of either the preceding or subsequent profane social statuses or cultural states" (Turner 1982, 24). The threshold situation is a moment of pure potentiality, in which "the past is momentarily negated, suspended, or abrogated, and the future has not yet begun . . ." (ibid. 44). In the final integration or incorporation symbolic actions are performed that stabilize the return to social life with reference to the liminal experience.

Besides the aspect of liminality, rituals are fed by the moment of con-trafactuality; in this interplay the supposed normativity of the factual is disturbed and alternative views of the life of the world and of relation-ship to God are set in place. Consequently, rituals do not simply imitate the experience of reality. Instead, they embody in stylized form, through use of the imagination and imitation, one's *own* reality. "Ritual is not imitation, but the momentary sense of what is not. Ritual mimesis creates its own referentiality" (Bahr, 1998, 154).

"Wash me clean of my misdeeds."
An Example of a Purification Ritual

The following example may illustrate how such a staging of counter-realities in liminal space can take place, whereby the experience of pollution is transformed into another sense-context. I am not in the first instance pursuing any interest in enlightenment or effort to refute the experience of impurity with a demonstration that it represents an in-appropriate, premodern idea of illness. Instead, the symbolic world of impurity will be taken up and reinhabited. Only in this way can the experience of those affected truly be taken seriously.

Pastor A accompanied Mrs. B for over two years in regularly sched-uled pastoral conversations that often centered on the question of what encounters and experiences of exile from her homeland had led to her becoming dependent on drugs, being forced then to work as a prosti-tute, and finally being infected with HIV by one of her johns. She often spoke of others' guilt, until finally she was more and more possessed by the feeling that she experienced her whole past as dirty. The ques-tion of her own responsibility tortured her increasingly. She had not re-sisted heroin, and thus she had "dirtied" her body and her soul. Pastor A saw his task, in this phase of care, as supporting her and giving her permission, so to speak, to confront her own responsibility. As the tenth anniversary of the death of a good friend of hers neared, she felt an in-creasing need to be supported in remaining in a methadone program and not allowing her disastrous past to have the final word over her present life. Her life story revealed the approach of a transitional situ-ation that needed to be entered, through mutual agreement, in a wor-ship service.

From a theological point of view the worship service should be a re-membrance of baptism. Against their experience of feeling threatened by corrupting powers and finding their path a life-and-death struggle, these persons should encounter the assurance that through their bap-tism they have been wrenched from the diabolical forces and that a change of rulership has taken place in them. Belonging to Christ means standing before him as "clean." Belonging to the Body of Christ means shedding all dependence on the powers of this world. Baptism, the sacrament of liberation from the spell of evil, is both a unique event and a lifelong process. Mrs. B, who could scarcely remember that she had been baptized, needed to be reassured that her life, too, was grounded in the "water of rebirth" (Titus 3:5).

Mrs. B, because of her feelings of shame, did not want to make the ritual that was being planned for her accessible to the public. For this reason the two agreed that she would take responsibility for writing a text that would situate her feelings of pollution within her life story. They met a week later, first in a vestibule of the chapel. Mrs. B was in party dress. This first phase served to separate her from daily routine and slow down the pace of time. Why do you come here today? What do you wish? Are you excited? After these preparations, they moved into the chapel and Pastor A put on his cassock. After the reading of the plea from Psalm 51: "Wash me thoroughly from my iniquity, and cleanse me from my sin," Mrs. B read the testimony she had composed about the "soiling" she had experienced in her life and her desire to be cleansed. This highly tense emotional moment was sustained by music that followed, and in which she could allow her tears to flow freely. Pastor A gave thanks for her courage to see clearly, and responded to her confession of guilt with Psalm 32:

> Happy are those whose transgression is forgiven,
>   whose sin is covered.
> Happy are those to whom the LORD imputes no iniquity,
>   and in whose spirit there is no deceit.
> While I kept silence, my body wasted away
>   through my groaning all day long.
>   . . .
> I said, 'I will confess my transgressions to the LORD,'
>   and you forgave the guilt of my sin.

In these words of the psalm the description of pollution is answered with the promise of forgiveness imaged as washing. The silent adherence to evil, which causes the wasting of the body, and then the separation from evil are both decisively named.

So the phase of transformation was begun. The promise of forgiveness of sin as an act of purification made possible the mimetic presentation of a counter-reality strengthened and given sensual expression by the subsequent washing and anointing. As she washed her hands in flowing water caught by the baptismal font she separated herself from the "dirt" in her life, which no longer had power over her.

The purification was followed by an anointing of the forehead, eyes, ears, lips, hands, and feet as a sign of the strengthening and dignifying of her body and its senses. The things she had experienced through these senses could not be made not to have happened, but they could be disempowered. In her body, too, a new reality was to be inscribed, a reality that would give her the strength to go on. In this sense Pastor A blessed her. Then the church door was opened. Mrs. B took the bowl with the water, cried aloud, and flung its contents into the street. The moment of the disempowerment of evil, which was of central significance in this worship service, found another expression in this spontaneous, powerful gesture by the woman herself.

Unbelievable things can happen on the borders if the words of Sacred Scripture are inscribed in the body through ritual. Transgressors thus become witnesses to the exorcistic and healing power of the Gospel, which transforms the world in spite of all resistance.

Bibliography

Bahr, Petra. "Ritual und Ritualisation. Elemente zu einer Theorie des Rituals im Anschluß an Victor Turner," *Praktische Theologie* 33 (1998) 143–58.

Brix, Klaus. "Das seelsorgerliche Gespräch mit HIV-Infizierten und AIDS-Kranken," in Sozialmedizinisch-Psychologisches Institut der Ev.-Luth. Landeskirche Hannovers, ed., *Ergänzungsheft zur Mappe: Leben mit AIDS.* Hannover, 1994, 16–22.

Christiansen, Nils. "'Aber ich darf den Herrn Pastor doch nicht stören!' Seelsorge baut Gemeinde," *Lernort Gemeinde. Zeitschrift für Gemeindebildung* 16 (1998) 61–64.

Christiansen, Nils, and Bertold Höcker. "Neue Formen des Gedenkens," in *12 Jahre Aids-Hilfe Kiel e.V.: 1986–1997*. Kiel, 1998, 46–49.

Douglas, Mary. *Purity and Danger: An Analysis of Concepts of Pollution and Taboo.* London: Routledge & Kegan Paul; New York: Praeger, 1966.

Gennep, Arnold van. *Les rites de passage; étude systématique des rites de la porte et du seuil, de l'hospitalité, de l'adoption, de la grossesse et de l'accouchement, de la naissance, de l'enfance, de la puberté, de l'initiation, de l'ordination, du couronnement des fiancailles et du mariage, des funérailles, des saisons, etc.* Paris: E. Nourry, 1909. English: *The Rites of Passage.* Translated by Monika B. Vizedom and Gabrielle L. Caffee. Introduction by Solon T. Kimball. London: Routledge & Kegan Paul; Chicago: University of Chicago Press, 1960.

Jarchow, Rainer. *Leben durch Aids. Anstöße und Erfahrungen des Aids-Pastors.* Stuttgart, 1996.

Kriener, Manfred. "UN=Offizielle sprechen erstmals von der Pest," *die tageszeitung* June 29, 1998.

Langer, Susanne K. *Philosophy in a New Key: A Study in the Symbolism of Reason, Rite and Art.* Cambridge, Mass.: Harvard University Press, 1942.

Luther, Henning. "Tod und Praxis. Die Toten als Herausforderung kirchlichen Handelns," *ZThK* 88 (1991) 407–26.

Major, Stefan. "Positiv im zweiten Jahrzehnt. Über das Leben von HIV-Infizierten in der Bundesrepublik," *Pro Familia Magazin* 6 (1995).

Sontag, Susan. *AIDS and Its Metaphors.* New York: Farrar, Strauss and Giroux, 1989.

Turner, Victor. "Liminal to Liminoid, in Play, Flow, Ritual: An Essay in Comparative Symbology," in idem, *From Ritual to Theatre: The Human Seriousness of Play.* New York: Performing Arts Journal Publications, 1982.

Wilhelm Schwendemann

God's Answer to Job

> *"Or who shut in the sea with doors*
> *when it burst out from the womb?—*
> *when I made the clouds its garment,*
> *and thick darkness its swaddling band,*
> *and prescribed bounds for it,*
> *and set bars and doors,*
> *and said, 'Thus far shall you come, and no farther,*
> *and here shall your proud waves be stopped'?"*
>
> (Job 38:8-11)

Job the Transgressor

Suffering, whether experienced personally or as sympathy with the suffering of another, is always a challenge to our beloved image of God. The ideas about God we formed in childhood are massively called into question by suffering, which forces us to a more mature, developed view of God if we are not to lose faith in God altogether. Job, the protagonist of the biblical book of the same name, is that kind of transgressor between different images of God. In the course of the story he abandons his old view of God, still clearly expressed by his wife and his three friends and corresponding to spontaneous human reaction to the experience of suffering. God responds to Job in a speech that opens for Job a new, liberating notion of God and the world. In this essay, following the chronology of the biblical events, I want to concentrate on the significance of God's answer to Job.

The book of Job, a masterpiece of Hebrew poetry, is placed among the Wisdom literature of the Bible. An extensive dialogue is set within a brief narrative framework (Job 1–2; 42:7-17). The framing story in Job 1 and 2 begins with the pious, righteous, rich, healthy man Job being put to the test as a result of an agreement between God and Satan made in a kind of heavenly council. The misery that breaks over this man, then, is profound. He loses his wealth, all his possessions, his children, and his health.

In the dialogue portion (Job 2:11–27:23) three friends, Eliphaz, Bildad, and Zophar, and later another friend, Elihu, visit Job and try to console him by interpreting his suffering for him. Job's cursing of himself (Job 3) precedes the dialogue. Job refuses consolation and in his misery casts imprecations on himself. The series of dialogues ends with a praise of Wisdom in ch. 28, followed then by Job's further internal dialogues and laments in chs. 29–31 and Elihu's speeches in chs. 32–37. God's two speeches and Job's responses in 38:1–42:6 conclude the poetic portion of the book.

In the conclusion of the framing narrative in Job 42:7-17 God criticizes Eliphaz and the other two friends because they did not speak rightly of God, whereupon Job enters pleas on their behalf. Job is justified, recovers his health, and again becomes rich and fruitful (begetting three daughters, Jemimah, Keziah, and Keren-happuch, with rights of inheritance, as well as seven sons). The story closes with a "happy ending": Job dies old and full of years.

A Wife Can Also Be Mistaken

Job's wife has a key position in the intensifying drama. Branded by her unhappiness, she urges Job to blasphemy: he should curse God and take leave of this hand-me-down God (Job 2:9, 10). But if he did so, Job would have set in motion a juridical process (Lev 24:16) that could only end in death for him and for his wife. In the history of the exegesis of the book of Job this passage has often been interpreted misogynistically (Satan in the guise of the woman). Another viewpoint emerges if one considers the state of communication between the couple. Job's wife has to react cynically because she is as much in despair as Job, which distorts her perception of reality. She is trying to rid herself of the image of the powerful, tyrannical-male God, even though her attempt goes awry. The background for her idea of God is the so-called cause-and-effect scenario, according to which optimistic and naïve attitudes to life presume that blessing, happiness, and wealth are the results of right obedience to God. Misery, illness, etc. are, on the other hand, consequences of sinful behavior. In order not to surrender to despair Job again becomes a transgressor, distancing himself internally from his wife and clinging to his image of a just God.

Despair Becomes Cursing

After Job has endured his suffering for days, almost mute, in the third chapter he opens his mouth to scream out his misery. He breaks out of his reserve and silence, creates a free space in which he can confront

God with his distress. Every part of Job's cursing of himself (similarly to Jer 20:14-18) has its own theme. Job curses the beginning of his life, he curses the day of his birth and laments that he did not die on the day he was born; he wishes that his life of suffering and doubt had never existed. Thus in a transferred sense he curses the beginning of creation itself. The chaos that threatens creation is evoked by Job in the image of the darkening of the day, for example through the sun's eclipse. Night becomes a metaphor for threat, for chaos. In the Hebrew text the night is also called "curser of the day," something that is able to awaken the chaotic being Leviathan. In 3:11 curse becomes lament. In 3:12 the image of "knees to receive" appears to refer to a ritual of adoption: the accept-ance of an obligation to care for the infant is expressed in legal symbols, as one takes the child in one's lap or puts it to the breast. Here in v. 12 the reference seems to be to motherly care. In death all care ceases, but also distress and restlessness. Verses 14-16 say that death comes to each; it hastens toward and casts down even the powerful, the rulers of the earth. In v. 22 Job awaits death no longer as a friend, but simply as the hope of the despairing. At the end of the third chapter Job is de-picted as a worn out man, *in extremis* and despairing.

Again Job passes beyond the boundaries of his image of God: in cursing his existence he makes God responsible for his misery. Then it is not Job who, as the cause-and-effect scheme pretends, is responsible for his fate, but God. God, who created Job's life, is thus also the initiator of his unhappiness—a thought almost unique in the Hebrew Bible, but one that pervades the whole Job poem.

Well-Intended Pastoral Care and Its Consequences

Between the friends and Job develops a profound dialogue in which, certainly, the gaps and lack of understanding between the dialogue partners grow greater and greater. Job's friends fail in their efforts to console him with their wisdom because they insist on the cause-and-effect scheme and are unwilling to recognize Job as a suffering right-eous man. The goal of the wisdom and wise instruction of the friends is to show Job a correct understanding of life. What I am calling "wisdom" here is a phenomenon of antiquity, often appearing in other cultures as well, that can be regarded as a "theology of practical reason." Wisdom in this sense is practical knowledge about life and daily existence. Wisdom poetry aims at appropriate behavior in daily life or the right knowledge of such life. In the human wisdom of Ancient Near Eastern antiquity the object is to learn, practice, and hand on the art of living and surviving in ordinary life in the presence of dangers, crises, catas-trophes, death, and unlove. The cause-and-effect scheme, oriented almost completely to male ways of thinking and living, arises out of this kind of understanding of wisdom and intends both a pedagogical motivation of people to ethically good actions and a deterrent to socially damaging bad actions. The Good is the principle of divine creation, the Bad is the principle of chaos, the unworld, the uncreation. The Sumerians called this primeval order *Me*, the Egyptians *Maat*, the Israelites *Tsedaqah/* righteousness.

The wisdom of the three friends includes a fundamental trust in God's goodness and the righteousness of creation. Hence in their instructive pastoral care of Job they try to show that he must have committed some serious faults in his life. But in the book of Job this idea is fundamentally challenged and set right. Job despairs of God because he trusts in God's righteousness and hopes in a way that goes beyond the limits of the cause-and-effect scheme, but at first he receives no answer except to make God responsible for his misery. Therefore the friends, and even Job's wife, must fail: the friends because they call on Job to trust in the God of cause and effect, and his wife because she suggests to him that he should denounce the cause-and-effect God.

A Different God-Image

Beyond the God-images of Job's friends, his wife, and even of Job himself, in the first so-called divine speech in chs. 38–39, which is more like a hymn than a response to Job, there appears a different image, a divine counterimage associated not with death but with life. Job's idea of God is dis-placed for a third time: first there was the farewell to the fixed pattern of cause and effect, then the departure from the reductionist, despairing image presented by his wife; now he is called to reject the God who threatens and brings ruin. There is a close connection between the colorful images in chs. 38 and 39 and the dark and depressing images in chs. 2 and 3, because it is a question of neither reducing God's reality nor regarding it as irrelevant: neither painting it in black and white nor allowing oneself to be taken over by alienation from God, by sin, death, and the devil.

Can Job preserve his identity in view of his world in collapse? As late as the dialogue with Elihu he has experienced himself as not yet identical with his fate, and God as still standing apart. In ch. 3 Job laments that God's whole creation is inimical to life. God's plan is obscured. Job's reproach to God centers on his description of his own fate: because the one man, Job, is in severe difficulty, all creation is in chaos. The whole book of Job focuses on the connection between the recognition of one's own suffering and the "wisdom" in God's "plan of creation."

God's Irritating Answer to Job

What is God's response to Job in the hymn? God speaks, using the authentic divine name, out of a whirlwind (38:1-3) in a divine epiphany. (For the divine name see also the frame of the book and cf. 2 Kgs 2:1-11; Ezek 1:4; Exod 19:16-20.) God thus becomes the powerful subject of the discourse and not merely the object of Job's or his friends' philosophizing. Of course the whole discourse can be understood as a demonstration of God's power (as Hesse writes in his commentary). God does not respond directly to the situation Job is complaining about, but instead points to the whole of creation.

In what follows, so as to underscore the revolutionary character of this section, I will focus on the images and metaphors in the first discourse, concentrating on 38:8-11, which I have chosen as the epigraph for this essay.

In the first verses of ch. 38 Job is described as a man who obscures God's "plan" (a reversed presentation of his lament in ch. 3). God is thus not concerned about a single individual; the whole creation is at issue. Is there a plan within creation, or is it ruled by a (mythically colored) chaos inimical to life? Job's suffering is only mentioned because he has made his own fate the standard for judgment. Nevertheless, his questioning is not simply dismissed, but is in a certain sense taken up by God in that God challenges Job to a "fight."

God expects Job to recognize the fact that the finite cannot understand, comprehend, and judge the infinite. God has planned the world as one might plan a building, thus revealing God's creative action, and the divine way of working is not only creative, but also innovative and preserving. Humans cannot comprehend the continuum of time and space. What, then, can Job really "know" or understand? Verses 4-7 express in impressive fashion, and in contrast to the creation myths in Genesis, an idea of creation and the world not primarily oriented to human beings but issuing in cosmic jubilation. There is good reason to see the genre of ch. 38 as not only a hymn, but in fact a hymn of God and for God.

Verses 8-11 hymn the taming of the ocean's chaos; that is, God limits the sea's violent power. What is truly astonishing in these verses is how lovingly God approaches both the chaos and the creation itself, caring for the created universe as if it were a tiny infant.

In accord with God's ordering, vv. 12-15 sing of the dawn's light. Creation is renewed every morning and it is made clear to Job that he is not the ruler of space, time, and light. This (textually difficult) part of the hymn describes the relationship among creation, law, and power. Does Job really know the dimensions of the world (vv. 16-21)? There is a clearly ironic undertone to God's speech, but its effect is rather instructive than destructive. Further questions about origins and purpose follow. God's creative work appears as a masterpiece but, again in contrast to Genesis 4, it is not anthropocentric. Creation by its nature withdraws from utility and cannot be made utilitarian by human beings. The world is greater than anything the human can understand, and it was not created with an eye to the requirements of human institutions.

The last part of the hymn in ch. 38 draws attention to a cosmic event (weather, time) that is founded solely on God's ordinance. The series of animals in the last part of ch. 38 and the first verses of ch. 39 is made up entirely of carnivores, hunters who live lives entirely different from those of human beings, constituting a kind of counter image to human civilization. God cares even for the wild beasts by providing the kind of food they need (in contrast to the utopia in Isaiah 11)!

What Do Swaddling Clothes Mean in God's Creation?

The Bible mentions swaddling clothes three times (Ezek 16:4; Job 38:9; Luke 2:7). No biblical lexicon or dictionary has an article on swaddling. If we interpret Job 38:9 against the background of Ezek 16:4 we get the following image: After its birth an infant must have its umbilical cord cut, be washed in warm water or rubbed with oil (or, in an ancient Bedouin ritual, with salt), warmed, cared for, and wrapped in swaddling clothes or diapers. These are deeply human and almost self-evident actions. If they are omitted, we feel that such neglect is gross, violent, loveless, and humanly degrading. In Job 38, God cares for the created order, the whole of creation, just as a human person would care for a helpless newborn infant. God thus, through the "merciful" attentions that support newborn life, "rescues" creation, including all its component creatures (not leaving out the chaotic elements like the sea, the dragon of chaos, Leviathan, Behemoth, etc.) from the threat of abandonment to death. The whole section (vv. 8-11) is peppered with actions that could be described as obvious human-parental acts on behalf of an infant (protection through closing of the doors, exit from the mother's womb [*reḥem*], dressing, diapering, setting protective bars and doors). The only thing confusing in this section is the set of metaphors for the mythical and cosmic. Given the corresponding content of chs. 3 and 38 it seems very likely that Job's cursing of his own birth is being neutralized by the statements about the infant. The ritual of adoption described in ch. 3 is repeated in the metaphor of the swaddling clothes. The statement stands: God cares like a loving mother, a loving father (though the Hebrew *reḥem* in v. 8 points primarily to the actions of a mother) for creation in all its members. The motherly image of God hinted at here points far beyond the more male-oriented concept of God implied in the cause-and-effect pattern.

Job responds to these divine speeches rather curtly in Job 40:3-5. He understands that God's creative love surpasses his own insight, but I have the impression that Job's reaction to the divine speech is more capitulation than conviction. Hence follow the second divine speech and Job's answer in 42:1-6, this time with reference to the knowledge gained in love (42:3, 6). The emphasis is not on God's creative actions (in my opinion Job 38 is repeatedly understood falsely in this sense) but on the understanding gained by Job (in ch. 42) on the basis of that love. The animal motifs point in this direction, as they move within a horizon of knowledge theory that is accessible to the human (for this, see the great didactic poem in Job 28).

Job accepts the new, liberating knowledge of God that is offered to him "with relief," and withdraws his curses and laments even though he still lies "in dust and ashes."

Lament Turns to Solidarity

Human beings are meant to find their way within a world that is not strange, but familiar to them. But God alone gives wisdom, which is even personified as *Lady* Wisdom. In the book of Job the limits of wisdom are indicated by the question: How can a wise person still recognize God as just, in light of the suffering of innocent people? Job rejects the arguments of his friends; for him, a God who permits unjust suffering is also unjust. God reveals God's own self to Job in the midst of this experience (Job 38:1–42:6). Theologically, we are facing the problem of theodicy (see Rom 3:4-5: Why do I suffer?). Human suffering is a scandal to reason. Job 38 shows that God has not taken leave of the world. God loves creation and cares for it as a mother cares for her child. Therefore human dealings with suffering cannot be emancipated or relieved of solidarity from one's own or others' suffering. The enduring of suffering is itself the key to open the experiential space in which the painful question of "why" is taken up by God's very self. Every rationalization or legitimation of suffering breaks out of the communicative situation of sym-pathy, suffering with, and prevents solidarity with those who suffer. Franz Kafka once said: "You can withdraw from the world's suffering; that is permitted you and corresponds to your nature. But it may be that this very withdrawal is the only suffering you could prevent" (quoted from Bühler 1996, 162).

The Bible has no words for the distanced attitude toward suffering that is so common in our society today. For the biblical author of Job 38–39 such an attitude is simply unimaginable.

Bibliography

Brüning, Christian. "Kleine Schule des Staunens," *Erbe und Auftrag* 72/5 (1996) 385–413.

Bühler, Christian. "Hiob. Ein Zugang für die Sekundarstufe II," *Der Evangelische Erzieher* 48/2 (1996) 162–78.

Ebach, Jürgen. *Streiten mit Gott – Hiob, Teil 2*. Neukirchen-Vluyn: Neukirchener Verlag, 1996.

Groß, Heinrich. *Ijob*. NEB 13. Würzburg: Echter, 1986.

Hausmann, Jutta. "'Weisheit' im Kontext alttestamentlicher Theologie. Stand und Perspektiven gegenwärtiger Forschung," in Bernd Janowski, ed., *Weisheit außerhalb der kanonischen Weisheitsschriften*. Gütersloh: Gerd Mohn, 1996, 9–19.

Hesse, Franz. *Hiob*. 2nd ed. Zürich: Theologischer Verlag, 1992.

Keel, Othmar. *Jahwes Entgegnung an Hjob. Eine Deutung von Hjob 38–41 vor dem Hintergrund der zeitgenössischen Bildkunst*. Göttingen: Vandenhoeck & Ruprecht, 1978.

Rad, Gerhard von. *Weisheit in Israel*. Neukirchen: Neukirchen-Vluyn, 1970. English: *Wisdom in Israel*. Translated by James D. Marton. London: S.C.M.; Nashville: Abingdon, 1972.

Ratschow, Carl-Heinz. *Atheismus im Christentum?* Gütersloh: Gerd Mohn, 1970.

Römer, Thomas. *La Sagesse dans l'Ancien Testament: Proverbes, Job, Qohéleth*. Aubonne: Editions du Moulin, 1991.

Schroer, Silvia. *Die Weisheit hat ihr Haus gebaut. Studien zur Gestalt der Sophia in den biblischen Schriften*. Mainz: Matthias-Grünewald, 1996. English: *Wisdom Has Built Her House*. Translated by Linda M. Maloney. Collegeville: The Liturgical Press, 2000.

Schüngel-Straumann, Helen. *Rûah bewegt die Welt. Gottes schöpferische Lebenskraft in der Krisenzeit des Exils*. Stuttgart: Katholisches Bibelwerk, 1992.

Bettina Eltrop

Problem Girls:
A Transgressive Reading of the Parable
of the Ten Virgins (Matthew 25:1-13)

When a transgressor woman, armed with the methods of historical criticism, feminist hermeneutics, and some unusual social-historical questions for the biblical text, sets out to make her way through this forest, she can certainly expect some surprises. Old familiar biblical texts reveal themselves in unsuspected ways. New treasures wait to be brought to light. The new path leads her over precious gems, but over stones for stumbling, too.

I want to report, in this essay, about such a stumbling block/precious stone in the New Testament that I discovered for the first time about four or five years ago. Some problem girls appear in this text, five of whom I would call transgressors. I have different reactions to them, alternating between anger and joy; at one point they are a stone that makes me stumble and then again they seem to me a treasure in the great field that is the Bible.

Precious Gem: A "Girl" Text in the New Testament

The occasion for my discovery of the "problem girls" was the dissertation I wrote a few years ago on children in the New Testament. In fact, the first time I read through the New Testament I did not perceive the parable about the ten virgins in Matt 25:1-13 as a "children" text. For me—perhaps under the influence of depictions in churches and medieval book illustrations—virgins were elderly-looking unmarried women, "old maids," or at best "young women," but certainly not children or girls.

This "gem" seems to be overlooked as a rule. Even Elaine M. Wainwright, who read Matthew's Gospel from a feminist perspective in her

163

1991 dissertation, did not include this parable in her investigation. Why is this? Speaking for myself, at least, I suspect that it is connected with the word "virgin" for women and girls, which in today's ears sounds fuzzy and unclear. Hence for me it was an important first step to understand what the word *parthenos* really meant 1900 years ago, and what portion of a woman's life and what conditions it described.

The Greek lexicons give a first impression: Bauer's dictionary translates *parthenos* as "virgin," and indicates that outside the New Testament *parthenos* appears with the meanings "virgin daughter," "sweetheart," "girl" (BAGD 627; see now BADG 777, which gives as the primary meaning "one who has never engaged in sexual intercourse, *virgin, chaste person*"). Liddell and Scott's dictionary contains an entry similar to that in BAGD, and shows that *parthenos* could describe both the girl (that is, her age) in terms of biological virginity and the status of being unmarried. In his examination of Jewish inscriptions Jean-Baptiste Frey came to the following conclusion: "The word *parthenos* simply describes a young girl, with no moral nuance. It is in the first place an indication of age: the person concerned is still quite young but has put childhood behind her. It is also an indication of a social situation: this person is not yet married" (Frey 1975, 1:cxvii).

The New Testament fits completely within this group of findings: in Matthew *parthenos* appears in the parable of the ten virgins (Matt 25:1-13), and otherwise only in the infancy narrative, in one part of the manuscript tradition for Matt 1:16 and in a quotation from Isaiah in Matt 1:23, as a description for Mary. Luke also applies the word *parthenos* to Mary, to describe the period of her betrothal, that is, the time before she was married and taken to her husband's house as well as her biological virginity (Luke 1:27, 34). Luke also knows that the prophet Anna was a virgin *(parthenos)* when she married (2:36). In Acts 21:8-9 it is clear that a *parthenos* obviously lives in her father's house: Philip's seven daughters, "virgins who prophesied," live in his house.

In 1 and 2 Corinthians Paul distinguishes a *parthenos* from two other groups of women who are also unmarried. While the *parthenos* is evidently an untouched, pure girl who *will* be married (2 Cor 11:2), Paul is also aware of unmarried women/girls who may themselves choose to marry. In 1 Cor 7:36 Paul refers to the *parthenos hyperakmos* or "overage virgin" who of her own will may marry *(gameitoōsan* in this verse is third person plural *active*). This seems to be about emancipated, that is, grown daughters/virgins who are past the age of being married off by their fathers (twelve and a half) and thus are independent of them. In 1 Cor 7:34 Paul distinguishes the *gynē agamos* or unmarried woman from the virgin *(parthenos)*. At that time an unmarried woman could be a girl or woman who was unmarried, but had passed the age of twelve and a half and was therefore an independent adult (like the *parthenos hyperakmos*). In addition, the phrase *gynē agamos* describes a woman who had been married but had received a decree of divorce and thus was no longer under the control either of her father or of her husband, or she could be a widow who had children (sons?) and so did not fall under the obligation of levirate marriage. All these three life situations, any of which could occur at a very early time in a woman's life, coincide in the fact that such women were independent, could act autonomously, and were not subordinated to a man (husband or father). (See the further material in Wegner 1988, 14–22; Eltrop 1996, 38–47.)

Ideally, then, at that time a *parthenos* was a not-yet-married girl under the age of twelve and a half years, still dependent on her father as regards marriage, and at the same time a "biological virgin," a "girl," and "unmarried." The ten virgins in the parable in Matt 25:1-13 were in all probability ten unmarried, untouched young girls, approaching puberty as we would say nowadays.

The Reign of God and the Wedding's Perfume

Ten girls thus stand at the center of a parable, a narrative told in the context of an oriental wedding. They walk, sleep, discuss, and act, and their actions, the text says, are immediately transparent to the *basileia*, the reign of God: "Then the kingdom of heaven will be like this. Ten virgins [or: bridesmaids] took their lamps and went to meet the bridegroom" (Matt 25:1).

This group of girls is thus going to meet the bridegroom, the husband of the bride (their friend?). Their task is to accompany him on the way to the bride's house, or rather the bride's father's house, and to light the way for him (vv. 1-6, 10); perhaps they will even dance a wedding dance with their burning torch-lamps. This walk that the girls in the parable illuminate and accompany is the last stage in a marriage, which at that time began with the betrothal and concluded about a year later when the bridegroom brought the bride into his house. The parable seems to describe such a bringing-home of the bride. The virgins with their lamps are supposed to go with the groom as he walks to the house of the bride's father.

The virgins seem to be deliberately mentioned here, because this is more than a courtesy to the groom, more than simply lighting his way in the darkness. Men or servants could have done that, especially as darkness was falling. The choice of ten virgins indicates something about the social significance of this ritual. The ten *parthenoi*, as we know from what we have seen about the meaning of the word, are apparently similar to the bride in age and social status, and their function is to accompany the husband-to-be on the last stretch he travels to the house of the bride's father in order to bring home his bride. They enter the house with the groom and remain in the bride's father's house as part of the wedding party during the festive wedding celebration (vv. 10-11).

We know from many other New Testament passages that the "kingdom of heaven" has something to do with a wedding, with invitation and the abundance and rejoicing of a great, joyful festival; but that it also has something to do with the behavior of ten young girls during a ritual part of the festival, and with the aroma and light of their burning torch-lamps in the dark night—that is something we may discover as a new gem within the biblical message.

Stone of Stumbling:
Foolish Girls and Wise Girls (Matt 25:2)

Our initial joy at discovering ten young girls as the principal actors in a parable about the reign of God is quickly dampened, for in the very next verse they are divided into two categories: "Five of them were foolish, and five were wise" (25:2). The next two verses explain why some were foolish and some wise: The foolish virgins only took their lamps with them, while the wise also took some oil. The transgressor woman who reads this begins to suspect that she is about to encounter a didactic piece about correct behavior for girls. After all, that is the kind of contrast we were brought up with: a good/well-behaved girl does this and that, or else doing or not doing so and so is improper for a well-behaved/good girl. Unfortunately, a good many hearers/readers submit to such polarizing and divisive depictions and forget that the world is not made up of black and white (wise and foolish girls), but there are also many shades of grey. The story gets still more annoying: the groom is late, and everything else in the story takes place because of his tardiness. Sure enough! The same old problem: the man is late, and it's the women's fault—no?

At any rate, the whole group of girls falls asleep. The community of exegetes sees in this description the situation of the Christian community, where the bridegroom was identified as Jesus, whom they believed God had raised and made Christ and Lord. The people wait and hope for his return, but the parousia is delayed; they have to wait longer than they had expected. People in the community gradually cease waiting for Jesus . . . or those who have prepared themselves well for Christ's coming can sleep in peace, because they are ready. According to this logic one group of virgins is wise because they have assessed the situation correctly, reckoning with the possibility that the bridegroom would come late. According to most interpreters this parable is really not about being awake (v. 13), but about being ready at all times.

They all fall asleep; it is the middle of the night. Then suddenly there is a cry: the bridegroom is coming! The girls wake and prepare their torch-lamps. At this point the "foolish" girls see that their oil will probably not last. In vv. 8 and 9 we find a dialogue between the two groups of girls that is worth looking at more closely:

> The foolish said to the wise, "Give us some of your oil, for our lamps are going out." But the wise replied, "No! there will not be enough for you and for us; you had better go to the dealers and buy some for yourselves."

The foolish girls ask the others for oil, but the wise girls refuse to share and recommend to the others that they go quickly to the marketplace and buy oil. Showing no solidarity with the girls who then in fact run to the market, the wise accompany the bridegroom into the house when he comes and celebrate the wedding feast while the others stand outside (vv. 10-12). And that kind of behavior is praised?

Problem Girls:
A Question About Our Own Image of Women and Girls

Wait a minute! What happened to the suspicion that the division of the group of girls into foolish and wise was supposed to reinforce a positive image of how girls should behave (in patriarchal societies)? After some reflection I note that *I* even want to impose this harmonizing good-girl behavior on the wise girls: sharing, being in solidarity— especially with other girls and women, even at cost to oneself. But that kind of accommodating and kind girl-behavior is just what the text does *not* praise! Is the Bible more progressive than I am?

The group of wise girls in the parable is not distinguished by characteristics that are typical of good, pliable girls. Instead, the wise show traits that have a more emancipatory character. It is not obedience, harmony, and selflessness that are called for, but shrewdness and right action, independence and taking responsibility for one's own acts— and this is required of girls, no less.

In Matthew's Gospel being wise/*phronimos* is frequently demanded in connection with discipleship (cf., for example, Matt 7:24; 10:16). It characterizes right action (7:24; 24:45; 25:2-12) and far-seeing action beyond the immediate moment (7:24-25; 25:4-12) as the kind of action required of Jesus' disciples. Matthew 7:24-27 in particular is very similar to this parable: it distinguishes between a wise man who builds his house on rock and a foolish man who builds his house on sand. While the first house withstands every storm, the second is swept away by the rain. Like the wise man in Matt 7:24-25, the wise girls in this parable are examples of the kind of action required of disciples of Jesus. They act wisely, prudently, and with reflection.

The girls' independence is especially evident in the dialogue. Here we find an amazingly "cool" way of arguing. The rejection of the demand in v. 9 shows a remarkably prudent eye to the future. They refuse solidarity with the other girls by saying that if they acceded, the supply of oil would not be sufficient for any of them. Their lack of readiness to share is thus well founded. The wise go on to recommend to the others a different solution to the problem: "go to the dealers and buy some for yourselves" (v. 9).

The parable is apparently intended to tell Jesus' disciples in the Matthean community: each of you can, like these young girls, enter the *basileia* or fail to enter it. All people, even young girls, are responsible for their actions, for their discipleship, and for their entry into the *basileia*.

Now I can live with this passage, more or less. But that the wise, through their actions, are nevertheless transgressors, walking the boundary between the decisiveness to say and do the right thing at the right time and unsolidary action—that is something that still bothers me about these problem girls. The stone of stumbling is beginning to shine a little, but my joy in it is still not entirely unclouded.

Unsolidary Action:
An Aid to Reading from Nicaragua

One of my favorite books about the Bible is *The Gospel in Solentiname,* edited by Ernesto Cardenal. In the dialogue of the simple peasants of Nicaragua about this parable I read how they see what I regard as the unsolidary behavior of the wise, and above all the role of the foolish:

> Oscar: We are all these ten girls, and just as there are five and five in this example, so there are some Christians who are for justice and others who are not. And when the bridegroom comes, those who go along with injustice want to quickly fill their lamps with love; but then it is too late . . .

> Laureano: There are young men who used to be revolutionaries, even guerillas, but then they regretted it. They are now so far from their earlier ideals that all they think about is earning money. I think they have also run out of oil.

Another Young Man: The gospel speaks of young girls, maybe because this parable is addressed especially to young people: It is the youth of humanity that waits with its lamp in its hand.

Olivia: The parable is for everyone, the old and the young. We older people also must keep hope alive, just like the young people.

Alejandro, her son: That is just why a young reactionary is really unforgivable.

Oscar: A young person whose oil runs out is really old. The light goes out, love is lost . . . he has no more light for the great feast (Cardenal 1980, 506–08).

When I read this dialogue it dawned on me that I myself had paid very little attention to the foolish girls until now. The farmers of Solentiname, however, drawing on their experience, had concrete people in mind: Christians who did not cooperate in working for more justice, whose earlier ideals had "burned out," and who now even worshiped the system of injustice, the mere gaining of money. And truthfully, when I look again at the dialogue and especially the first plea of the foolish, I see that it is not even a matter of a plea or a question, but a command, a demand: *Give us!*

Did the farmers in Solentiname sense better than I that among young Christians it must frequently be a question of staying alert in face of the others' demands?

God's Story Continues

What, then, does this example of the problematic/wise girls mean today? Maybe it means going bravely out into the darkness with the lamp, oil, and all spiritual supplies I still have, even if I and my own congregation have gotten very sleepy? and then letting myself be awakened and touched by the message, and acting and fighting responsibly—dancing a crackling torch dance with some women in the night and letting the others go their way? Should we entrust young people in our churches with more responsibility?

Perhaps we can translate the parable this way. But I want to remind us of the possibility that we should not accept the conclusion of the parable, which transforms the wedding feast into a judgment scene, and that we should go on reading this parable resistantly. Nikos Kazantzakis, for example, gives the parable a new ending:

"What would you have done, Nathanael, if you had been the bridegroom?" Jesus asked again, and slowly, persistently, his beseeching eyes caressed the cobbler's simple guileless face.

"I would have opened the door," the other answered in a low voice so that the old chief would not hear. He had been unable to oppose the eyes of the son of Mary any longer.

"Congratulations, friend Nathanael," said Jesus happily, and he stretched forth his hand as though blessing him. "This moment, though you are still alive, you enter Paradise. The bridegroom did exactly as you said; he called to the servants to open the door. 'This is a wedding,' he cried. 'Let everyone eat, drink, and be merry. Open the door for the foolish virgins and wash and refresh their feet, for they have run much.'" (Kazantzakis 1960, 217)

I myself think that the "wise," who are feasting with the bridegroom, would indeed plead on behalf of the other five girls, and with a convincing argument that "in our village we do not celebrate weddings behind closed doors" would move the bridegroom to reconsider. Or maybe they would suggest to him that they dance the wedding torch dance again with all ten girls, because after all, they had been practicing it for weeks, to dance at the wedding today.

Bibliography

Altweg, Leni. "Ärger mit den fünf törichten Jungfrauen. Die Drohung der verschlossenen Tür," in Karin Walter, ed., *Frauen entdecken die Bibel.* 5th ed. Freiburg, Basel, and Vienna: Herder, 1986, 139–44.

Arndt, William F., F. Wilbur Gingrich, and Frederick W. Danker. *A Greek-English Lexicon of the New Testament and other early Christian literature: a translation and adaptation of the fourth revised and augmented edition of Walter Bauer's Griechisch-deutsches Wörterbuch zu den Schriften des Neuen Testaments und der übrigen urchristlichen Literatur.* Chicago: University of Chicago Press, 1979. (BAGD)

Cardenal, Ernesto, ed. *Das Evangelium der Bauern von Solentiname: Gespräche über das Leben Jesu in Lateinamerika.* 4 vols. Gütersloh: Gerd Mohn, 1980. (German translation of *Evangelio in Solentiname.*)

Danker, Frederick W. *A Greek-English Lexicon of the New Testament and other Early Christian Literature.* Chicago: University of Chicago Press, 2000. (BADG)

Eltrop, Bettina. *Denn solchen gehört das Himmelreich. Kinder im Matthäusevangelium. Eine feministisch-sozialgeschichtliche Untersuchung.* Stuttgart, 1996.

Frey, Jean-Baptiste. *Corpus Inscriptionum Iudaicarum. Corpus of Jewish Inscriptions: Jewish Inscriptions from the Third Century B.C. to the Seventh Century A.D.* Volume 1, Europe. New York: Ktav, 1975.

Kazantzakis, Nikos. *The Last Temptation of Christ.* Translated by P. A. Bien. New York: Simon and Schuster, 1960.

Liddell, Henry George, and Robert Scott. *A Greek-English Lexicon with a Supplement. A New Edition by Henry Stuart Jones and Roderick McKenzie.* 9th ed. Oxford: Oxford University Press, 1940 (reprint 1968).

Linnemann, Eta. *Gleichnisse Jesu. Einführung und Auslegung.* 4th ed. Göttingen: Vandenhoeck & Ruprecht, 1966. English: *Jesus of the Parables: Introduction and Exposition.* Translated by John Sturdy. New York: Harper & Row, 1967.

Luz, Ulrich. *Das Evangeliun nach Matthäus (Mt 18–25).* EKK I/3. Zürich, Einsiedeln, and Cologue: Benziger; Neukirchen-Vluyn: Neukirchener Verlag, 1997.

Wainwright, Elaine M. *Towards a Feminist Reading of the Gospel According to Matthew.* BZNTW 60. Berlin and New York: Walter de Gruyter, 1991.

Wegner, Judith Romney. *Chattel or Person?: The Status of Women in the Mishnah.* New York and Oxford: Oxford University Press, 1988.

Author Biographies

Christiane Rösener, b. 1969. First academic degree in Protestant religion and Spanish. At work since 1997 on a dissertation on the subject of "Routes to a Feminist Intercultural Theology." "Luise Schottroff's theology has guided me from the beginning of my studies, but I first met her personally at a conference in 1996. Since at that time she agreed to direct my dissertation she has been ready at all times, far beyond the limits of the doctoral seminar, to give me inspiration for my work."

Stefanie Müller, b. 1971. First academic degree in German and Protestant religious education, Siegen and Kassel. Graduate fellow, State of Hesse. "Luise, I met Beruriah in the course of working on my first Staatsexamen essay under your direction, on 'The Image of the Pharisee in Matthew 23 and in Recent Jewish and Christian Literature.' She was the sole woman learned in Torah who is named in rabbinic literature. This was an interesting discovery, since 'Christians' often think that in the Judaism of that time women had no access to the Torah or to offices of leadership. So I took the opportunity offered by this book to learn more about this woman and to do some further research."

Beate Wehn, b. 1970. Studied German and Protestant religious education, Siegen and Kassel. Since 1997 assistant to Luise Schottroff at the University of Kassel, writing a dissertation on women's experiences of violence in the apocryphal Acts of Apostles. "I am indebted to Luise's sense for transgressive women outside the well-trodden paths of theology for reference to this segment of the largely unexplored history of women."

Dr. Claudia Janssen, b. 1966. Studied Protestant theology in Kiel and Marburg. Received her doctorate in 1996 with a dissertation on "Elizabeth and Anna: Two Resistant Older Women in the New Testament Period." She served her vicariate in the Hannover Landeskirche, and has been for several years a member of the colloquium on Feminist

Liberation Theology at the University of Kassel. Her scholarly curiosity leads her constantly forward in her search for Paul.

Marlene Crüsemann, b. 1953. Studied Protestant theology in Göttingen and Heidelberg. Vicar in the Baden Landeskirche, Karlsruhe. Work with families and independent theological writing and publishing on feminist and social-historical interpretation of the Bible. She has known Luise since the 1980s, in the context of the "Heidelberg Working Group for Social-Historical Interpretation of the Bible," and has been inspired by her since that time. She is completing a dissertation under Luise's direction, entitled "The Letters to Thessalonica and Just Judgment. Studies in Composition and Jewish-Christian Social History."

Dr. Dagmar Henze, b. 1963. Studied Protestant theology in Göttingen and was for many years spokesperson for the Göttingen Women's Research Project on the History of Women Theologians. Received her doctorate with a dissertation on the liberal theologian Carola Barth and the earlier women's movement in the period 1900–1933. From 1993 to 1997 graduate assistant to Luise Schottroff at the University of Kassel. She served her vicariate in Münden, Hannover, and since 1997 has been a pastor in the neighborhood of Göttingen. She is married and has one child.

Dr. Irene Dannemann, b. 1962. Works as a pastor in a congregation in Frankfurt. She was a member of the colloquium on Feminist Liberation Theology at the University of Kassel, where she wrote her doctoral dissertation on the "bad" women in Mark's gospel.

Sigrid Lampe-Densky, b. 1957. Studied Protestant theology in Göttingen. Participant in several feminist liberation theology Summer University sessions at the University of Kassel. Married; pastor in Hannover.

Dr. Luzia Sutter Rehmann, b. 1960. Studied theology in Basel and Montpellier. Received her doctorate in 1994 at the University of Kassel under the direction of Luise Schottroff. Her dissertation was entitled *"Geh, frage die Gebärerin." Feministisch-befreiungstheologische Untersuchungen zum Gebärmotiv in der Apokalyptik.* From 1987 to 1996 she directed the Women's Project of the Lutheran-Reformed Church in the city of Basel. At present she is working with a research project on sexuality in early Christianity. She is the mother of two daughters.

Sigrun Wetzlaugk, b. 1968. Studied Protestant Theology and Art in Kassel and Göttingen. Participated in the establishment of the Archive for Feminist-Liberation Theology in Kassel. Since passing her examinations she has been at work on the biblical traditions of women's resistance and also writing a dissertation under the working title: "Schaffe mir Recht! Die widerständige Witwe in Lk 18:1-8: Gebet und Gerechtigkeit." She lives in Kassel with her husband and two children.

Dr. Ivoni Richter Reimer is the mother of Daniel (9) and Tiago (4), and married to Haroldo. She received her doctorate under Luise Schottroff's direction with a dissertation on the subject of "Women in the Acts of the Apostles" (*Women in the Acts of the Apostles: A Feminist-Liberation Perspective* [Minneapolis: Fortress, 1995]). She is a pastor in the Lutheran community of Niterói/Rio de Janeiro, Brazil, and lecturer in New Testament in the Bennett Methodist theological school, Rio de Janeiro. She is the Latin American Adviser for Human Rights of the Lutheran World Federation and member of the National Coordination of the Centro de Estudos Bíblicos (CEBI).

Dr. Choon-Ho You-Martin studied pharmacy and Protestant theology in Seoul, South Korea. In 1994 she received her doctorate at the University of Heidelberg. She is lecturer in the Presbyterian College and Theological Seminary in Seoul. Her research concentrates on Pauline theology, feminist hermeneutics, Korean feminist liberation theology, intercultural dialogue, ecumenics, the processes of modernization and globalization in the developing world, world religions, and new religious movements.

Eske Wollrad is a lesbian feminist cultural theologian with a doctorate in womanist theology. Her book on the concept of wildness in the work of Delores Williams was published by Gütersloh in the fall of 1999. "What I love most about Luise is her refusal to ignore those who wear very different chains from hers. At the Kirchentag in Leipzig, Luise said the words 'lesbian and gay love' before five hundred people. It is testimonies to solidarity like those that we will go on telling, in memory of her."

Ulrike Metternich, b. 1957, Protestant theologian and mother of three children, works as a pastoral vicar in Lörrach. Her research interests are in feminist theological interpretation of the New Testament miracle traditions. In November 1998 she received her doctorate under Luise Schottroff's direction with a dissertation entitled: "'Sie sagte ihm die ganze Wahrheit.' Eine feministisch-befreiungstheologische Exegese der Erzählung von der "Blutflüssigen" (Mk 5,25-34 parr.) auf dem Hinter-

grund einer sozialgeschichtlichen Untersuchung der Menstruations-
vorschriften im Judentum und frühen Christentum," to be published
soon.

Martina S. Gnadt, b. 1957, pastor with responsibilities for religious
instruction and pedagogical theory of religious education at the Frö-
belseminar, University of Kassel. "Luise Schottroff and I have known
each other since she began teaching in Kassel. A mutual friend introduced us because he thought we had 'a lot to say to each other.' That
has proved true now for over ten years. Teacher, doctoral thesis director, friend, and trusted companion has she been to me. She is a brave,
courageous, humorous, sympathetic, combative comrade on the road,
and without any doubt a transgressive woman."

Hanna Kreisel-Liebermann, b. 1955 in Schömberg/Calw, grew up in
Lüneburg. Studied theology and political science 1974–1981. Recipient
of a Villigst fellowship; vicar; gave religious instruction from 1986 to 1988
at the high school level; program director of the Heimvolkshochschule
Locum 1989–1990; lecturer in feminist theology and "bibliodrama" in
the Protestant Faculty of Theology at Hannover 1987–1991. Pastor of a
city church in Göttingen 1991–1997. Member since 1995 of the doctoral
seminar at Kassel. Since 1997 hospital chaplain; since 1998 in the research project SUPPORT of the Federal Department of Health at the
University of Göttingen. Married with three sons aged 22 to 14.

Dr. Andrea Bieler, b. 1963, received her doctorate in 1993 at the University of Kassel with a dissertation on the theologian Anna Paulsen,
thanks to the active support of her doctoral directors, Luise Schottroff
and Hannelore Erhart. At present she is Assistant for Practical Theology in the theological faculty of the Georg-August-Universität Göttingen, and Inspector in the theological seminary. Her Habilitation project
is concerned with the culture of Jewish and Christian preaching in the
context of the conflict between religion and modernity. Her further
interests include bibliodrama, feminist theological perspectives in
practical theology, and the Argentine tango.

Dr. Wilhelm Schwendemann is married to the social-work specialist
Christine Blum-Schwendemann; they have three children. He is professor of Protestant theology (First Testament) and religious pedagogy in
the schools (didactics) at the Protestant Technical University of Freiburg
in the faculty for Social Work, Diaconal Service, and Religious Education. His publications include theology, ethics, diaconal service, and

religious education (emphasis: media). He earned his doctorate in 1994 under the direction of Luise Schottroff and Hannelore Erhart with a dissertation on Calvin's theology and biblical interpretation.

Dr. Bettina Eltrop was born in Kassel in 1961. She is married and has three children. "I met Luise after completing my studies in Bonn (Catholic theology, biology, education, and philosophy for the Staatsexamen). Then I moved to Kassel, with two small children, to live with my parents so that I could hear the feminist theologians who were then teaching in the University at Kassel: Luise Schottroff, Dorothee Sölle, and Helen Schüngel-Straumann. The private and yet open character of these women's lectures and seminars, especially Luise's openness for new forms of communication (in the Summer University) and unconventional paths powerfully influenced my future course. The fact that I, as a woman student, had small children was, for example, no obstacle to a doctorate as far as Luise was concerned; instead, it was the hermeneutical starting point: I wrote my dissertation on children in Matthew's Gospel.

"One final, personal word to you, Luise: I am especially grateful, after all these years, for your helping me to the 'discovery of slowness,' which is a great help to me in my present profession. Thank you!"

Index of Subjects

Acts of the Christian Martyrs, 68, 69
Agunah, bound wife, 69
AIDS patients
    Hamburg Pastorate for AIDS Care, 145, 148
    isolation of, 148
    pastoral care of, 149
    rituals used in care of, 149–52

boundaries
    intercultural, transgressed by Ruth and Naomi, 2–3
    transgressing, 67
    looking closely at, 145
    wholesome aspect of some, 77–78
    See also Schottroff, Luise

cancer patients
    palliative care of, 139
    pastoral accompaniment of, 139–43
    quality of life of, 137–38
coexistence
    difficulties of, 7
    of Ruth and Naomi, 3–7. *See also* boundaries: intercultural
"Come and see," 40, 44, 45
confession of faith, 56–57

Dynamis
    in Mark, 5:25-34, 123
    in Paul, 123–24
    in Synoptics, 122
    in women, 124–25

faith of the Samaritan people, 42
fence. *See* boundaries: transgressing

Hagazussa, 67
"historical imagination," 62

Job
    friends' answer to, rejected, 157–58
    God's answer to, irritating but accepted, 159–60

Kashruth, food laws of Judaism. *See* Peter and Cornelius
Ketubah, 91
Konvivenz. See coexistence

levirate, 90
living water and liberation, 40–42. *See also* Samaritan woman

Minjung movement in South Korea. *See* women's theology

pain therapy, inadequate in developed countries, 138
parable of the ten virgins
    not about being awake, but about being ready, 167
    stumbling block in, being wise by not sharing is praised, 167–68
    See also parthemos
parthenos, 163–65
Paul
    feminist criticism of, in relation to Thecla, 21, 25
    the historical, 32–33
    lenses through which we have seen, 34–37
Pearl dealers in antiquity and early C.E. centuries, 59–63
Peter and Cornelius, 47–51
psalms, 81–82

Rabbi Beruriah, 9–16
repudium 69, 74–75
Ruth and Naomi, 1–8

Samaritan woman
    calling of, parallel to the disciples' in John 1:41-48, 40
    contrasting traditional and feminist interpretations of, 40
    first woman disciple and missionary, 40
    "left her water jar" and went to announce the Messiah, 40, 41
Seeing in John 9
    the blind man's, 132–33
    the disciples', 127–29
    Jesus', 130–31

Schottroff, Luise
    advice of, to her students, 121
    and boundaries, 67, 145
    feminist concept of leadership of, 44–45
    homage to, by students, 37, 53, 125
    profound influence of, on exegesis and hermeneutics, 15, 21, 40, 78, 83
selflessness. *See under* Schottroff, Luise: feminist concept of leadership
sin and punishment, 127–29, 157–59
stubborn widow
    "a little story of women's resistance to injustice" (Schottroff), 78
    a model for the behavior of all believers toward God and other human
        beings" (Schottroff), 83
    See also women's rights
Susanna's story, 26–27
swaddling clothes
    mentioned 3 times in Bible: Ezekiel 16:4; Job, 38:9; Luke 2:7, 160
    motherly image of God, 161

Thecla
    Acts of Thecla, 19, 28, 33–34
    apostle and teacher, 27–28
    and Paul, 20–23, 24
    similarities between, and Susanna, 27
transgressors. *See* boundaries

whiteness
    as depicted in the film "Dangerous Minds," 112–17
    as "one of the most efficient lies produced by modernity," 111
    as superiority on all levels, 111
widows
    injustice toward, 79, 81
    marginalized in Greco-Roman and Jewish societies, 77, 90
    See also stubborn widow; women's rights: fought for by a woman
wisdom, "theology of practical reason," 157
women merchants in antiquity and early C.E. centuries
    examples of, Lydia (Acts 16:4) and Priscilla (Acts 18:3), 63–64
    for, trade routes were also mission routes, 63–64
women's movements
    example of, in Brazil, 87–88
    example of, in South Korea, 97–99
women's rights
    defended by a man in John 8:1-11, 92–94
    fought for by a woman in Luke 18:1-8, 91–92

women's theology
  in South Korea, 103–8
  in the whole world, 108